THE BOOK OF THE LORD

The Great Awakening Volume XI

Sister Thedra

Copyright © 2021 by Halls of Light, LLC

All rights reserved. This book or any portion thereof may not be reproduced or used in any manner whatsoever without the express written permission of the publisher except for the use of brief quotations in a book review.

ISBN: 978-1-7366487-8-0

By Mine hand I have Blest this Book,
I dedicate it to All who seek the Light.

Contents

Mission Statement vi

EL-O-HEIM 17

THE PART OF COUNSEL 181

To the Reader

This book is only a portion of the teachings and prophecies that have been given by Sananda, Sanat Kumara, and others of the higher realms, and recorded by Sister Thedra.

Mission Statement

Give the truth to the world. Let it be received where it will. Many will read the messages. Some will accept the truth, others will read through curiosity, a few will ridicule. Yet to all is the truth given, and to all remains the power of choice.

The hope of the world in these times is in spiritualizing all forms of activity---promoting understanding through love and service. These must be the watchwords if the world is to come into lasting peace. We are trying to influence a world that is going astray and could cause undreamed of suffering. We are trying to overcome the thought of materialists and to bring a spiritual outlook into the earthly life. We need the help of all on earth who can think in spiritual terms. The great battle to be fought now is between the spiritual and the material, between idealism and carnalism. You can help by spreading the word---we are asking that you help because the battle may be long and the victory far away.

Halls of Light is not allied with any sect, denomination, political entity, organization, neither endorses nor opposes any cause. There are no dues for membership. Halls of Light is self-supporting through its own voluntary contributions. Halls of Light has but one purpose: to help through encouragement and understanding...

To contact the publishers or to obtain copies of our other books, please contact us at email: goldtown11@gmail.com

Esu Jesus Sananda

This reproduction is from an actual photograph taken on June 1st, 1961, in Chichen Itza, Yucatan, by one of thirty archaeologists working in the area at the time. Sananda appeared in visible, tangible body and permitted His photograph to be taken.

About the Late Sister Thedra

Since the later part of the last Century the Kumara wisdom preserved by Aramu Muru has begun to reemerge into the world. This process began with the late Sister Thedra, whom Jesus Christ appeared physically to while on her deathbed and spontaneously healed her of cancer while she was in the Yucatan, where she had gone to accept her fate, and the will of our Lord Jesus Christ. That is when something miraculous occurred.
Jesus spoke to her saying, "My name is Esu Sananda Kumara" and then sent Thedra down to the Monastery of the Seven Rays to learn the Kumara wisdom.
After five years, Thedra was told to return to the United States where she founded the Association of Sananda and Sanat Kumara at Mt. Shasta in California. While heading this organization, Thedra channeled many messages from Sananda and taught the Kumara wisdom until her passing in 1992.
While in the Yucatan it is said that while Sister during the 1960s Thedra was in the Yucatan, she was told a secret by her friend George Hunt Williamson, also known as Brother Philip, who authored Secrets of the Andes, and the SECRET PLACES OF THE LION. Williamson, confided in his long-time friend Sister Thedra that he intentionally scrambled the reincarnational lineages in order to protect this next generation when they the Mayan Solar Priests, who were the direct line descendants of the Kumara according to

prophesy were scheduled to reincarnate or return to fulfill their missions upon Earth, one of which was to relocate these ancient sites where the original records of the Amaru were placed for safe keeping.

Sister Thedra, 1900-1992, spent five years at the abbey undergoing intensive spiritual training and initiations. While in South America in the Yucatan, she had an experience which changed her in an instant when as it is told by her that Jesus Christ physically appeared to her and spontaneously cured her of cancer.

He introduced himself to her by his true, name, "Sananda Kumara," thereby revealing his affiliation with the Venusian founders of the Great Solar Brotherhoods. It was by his command that Sister Thedra went to Peru where in here travels she met Williamson. Sister Thedra eventually left Peru upon telling her experience there was complete.

Even before she returned to the States she met with harsh criticism from the church, which she elected to leave. (JW That was the church that is in Salt Lake City, Utah.)

She then traveled to Mt. Shasta in California and founded the Association of Sananda and Sanat Kumara. A.S.S.K.

You ask, Is There A Difference Between Jesus and Sananda?

Our Lords name given at birth by his father Joseph, and his beloved mother Mary was Yeshua, thus being of the house of David and the order of Yoseph, he would be called Yeshua ben Yoseph.

The Roman Emperors placed the name of Jesus upon the sir name of Yeshua, after the Emperor Justinian adopted Christianity as the official faith of Rome, and ordered that the sacred books be compiled, upon approval of a specially appointed council, appointed by the Emperor, into a recognizable and uniform work titled The Bible. Prior to this there never was a Bible per se.

There existed until the time of the Emperor's edict, a selection of many Sacred texts, that were employed in the Sacred Teachings. Many of which were copies of what the Greeks had transposed from the original texts in the Libraries of Alexandria, which were originally compiled by Alexander the Great, and were destroyed by Julius Caesar, fearing that they might prove dangerous to the rule of a Caesar, an Earthly God.
In addition, it kept. (he thought) the knowledge of Alexander's Libraries, out of the hands of the Ptolemy's, who were said to be descended from his bloodline.
At the time Caesar had no way of knowing the vast portions of the Library that were already in the Americas, in the Great Universities of the Inca, and the Maya.
Yeshua spent many years in the East after his ascension.
The good Sheppard, upon his appearances to the

Apostles after his ascension told his Apostles that he was in fact going to tend to his Father's other sheep; which means, plainly that he was continuing upon his sacred journey.

As the ascended one, Yeshua took to himself the name of Sananda, meaning the Christed one, and Sananda was thus embraced forever more by the Great Solar Brotherhood.

To many of you this is all new, to others it will be received as a welcome easing of the wall that has so long separated two sides of the same coin, this is being placed into the ethers and the matrix of thought at this time as it is the time of the Awakening, and the Christos is already emerging into the new consciousness, and mother Earth herself.

Sister Thedra and the phenomenon of channeling. Authority to use the name of Sananda was given to Sister Thedra when Jesus~ Sananda appeared to her in the Yucatan, and cured her instantly of the cancer that had taken her body over. Further, he allowed a picture of his countenance to be taken at that time that she might realize the occurrence was more than a dream. (JW I was told by my teacher and Guru Merelle Fagot that Thedra had a large format camera called a 620, if I remember right, and it had bellows on it and founded out. She used this to take the picture of Sananda. Merele said that she got some real good pictures with that camera. I have seen this picture that Thedra took and Sananda

didn't look very handsome, he just looked like a normal
person with not too long of hair and he had very dark skin.)
Sanada's Message to her by Sister Thedra.
"Sori Sori: Mine hand I have placed upon thine head,
and I have given unto thee the authority to use Mine
name. Give unto them the name Sananda, by which they
shall know Me as the Lord thy God - the Son of God, sent
that ye be made to know me, the One sent from out the
inner temple that there be Light in the world of men."
(The meaning of "Lord God: "The Lord God, for he is
"Lord" of, and responsible for, that which he has
brought forth.)
"Now it is come when ones which have the will to follow
Me shall come to know Me by that name which I commanded
thee to give unto the world as Mine "New name."
There are many that shall call upon the name of Jesus,
yet, they will deny the new name as they are want to do.
While unto thee I give assurance that I am the One sent
that there be Light in the world of men. Now let this
be understood, that they that deny Mine New Name deny
Me by any name. So be it I have appointed thee Mine
spokesman; I've given unto thee the power and authority
to speak for being that which I AM. And I say unto thee
Mine child whom I have called forth and anointed thee
with the Holy Spirit, thy name shall be as it is now
called, Thedra - that name I spoke unto thee from out
the ethers, and thou heard Me and accepted that which I
gave unto thee; and wherein have I deceived thee?
Wherein have I forgotten thee, or left thee alone?"
"I say unto thee, Mine hand is upon thee and I shall

sustain thee and you shall come to know that which I have kept for thee. So be it that I have kept thy reward, and at no time shall it be dissipated of scattered, for it is intact. So let this Mine Word suffice them which question thee - let them question, and I shall bear witness for thee. For do I not know
  Mine servants from the traitor?
Do I not reward Mine servants according unto their works or merits? I speak that they might know that I am mindful of Mine servants, that I am not a poor puny priest who has forgotten his servants."

"I say unto them, Mine servants shall be glorified above the crowned heads of the nations which have set themselves apart, and denied Me Mine part of Mine word for they have turned from Me in their conceit and forgetfulness."
"Now let this go on record as Mine Word, and I shall give unto them proof, which are of a mind to follow Me. So be it as I have spoken and I am not finished; I shall speak again and again, and I shall rise Mine Voice against them which set foot against Mine servants, and they shall be as ones cast out. So let them ask of Me and I shall enlighten them. So be it I know where of I speak. Be ye as ones blest to accept Me and know Me for that which I AM.
The Final Messages
On Saturday, June 13, 1992, at exactly 10.00 PM, at the age of 92, Sister Thedra made her final transition from the comfort of her own bed. When the time

arrived, she simply took one small breath and slipped quietly away, without pomp or fanfare.

She left as she had lived...as a humble servant for the greater good.

The messages that follow were given to Sister Thedra shortly before her transition.

They are compiled here to give you some idea of the significance of her passing and of the expansion of the work, as she is now free to work unencumbered by the physical limitations and by the pain which has so encumbered her in the past.

She has carried on the work here on the Earth plane for the last 50 years because that's where the work was needed...rest assured that her work now in the higher realms will simply be an extension of that work.

Sananda's Appearance

Be ye as one which hast heard Mine Voice and responded unto it - for I speak that ye hear, and I say that which is wise and prudent.

Let it be known that 1, the Lord thy God hast spoken and bear ye witness of Me, for I have made manifest Mineself that ye might know Me - and for this wast these manifestations made.

I say that I have made Mineself manifest that ye might see Me with thine mortal eyes; that ye might bear witness of Me. Yet thine companions saw and believed not; neither did they hear, for they were selfish and unprepared - yet, did I deny them?

I say; I came that they which would might see and hear. I went and came again unto Mine own. So be it that I have found; I have given unto the found that they which know not might know; that they might come to know as thou knowest.

Yet, how many hast turned from Me and persecuted thee for Mine Word. It is said, "Woe unto them which persecute Mine servants." is it not the law which they set into motion?

Yea Mine beloved, I say they bring about their own downfall. So be it that I am a compassionate one, and I would that they know what they do. So be it they shall learn well their lessons. So let it be, for this is the mercy of God, the One which hast sent Me.

So be it. I AM the Wayshower, the Lord thy God

I AM Sananda

Authority to Use the Name Sananda

Sori Sori: Mine hand I have placed upon thine head, and I have given unto thee the authority to use Mine name. For I first showed Mineself unto thee with the Word: "Go feed Mine sheep. Give unto them the name Sananda, by which they shall know Me as the Lord thy God - the Son of God sent that ye be made to know Me - the One sent from out the Inner Temple that there be Light in the world of men."

Now it is come when ones which have the will to follow Me shall come to know Me by that name which I commanded thee to give unto the world as Mine "New Name." There are many which shall call upon the name of Jesus, yet they will deny the New Name as they are want to do. While unto thee I give assurance that I am the One sent that there be Light in the world of men. Now let this be understood, that they which deny Mine New Name deny Me by any name. So be it I have appointed thee Mine spokesman; I've given unto thee the power and authority to speak for being that which I AM. And I say unto thee Mine child whom I have called forth and anointed thee with the Holy Spirit, thy name shall be as it is now called, Thedra - that name I spoke unto thee from out the eth, and thou heard Me and accepted that which I gave unto thee; and wherein have I deceived thee? Wherein have i forgotten thee, or left thee alone?

I say unto thee, Mine hand is upon thee and I shall sustain thee and ye shall come to know that which I have kept for thee. So be it that I have kept thy reward, and at no time shall it be dissipated or scattered, for it is intact. So let this Mine Word suffice them which question thee - let them question, and I shall bear witness for thee. For do I not know Mine servants from the traitor? Do I not reward Mine servants according unto their works or merits? I speak that they might know that I am mindful of mine servants, that I am not a poor puny priest who hast forgotten his servants.

I say unto them, Mine servants shall be glorified above the crowned heads of the nations which have set themselves apart, and denied Me Mine part of Mine Word - for they have turned from Me in their conceit and forgetfulness.

Now let this go on record as Mine Word, and I shall give unto them proof, which are of a mind to follow Me. So be it I have spoken and I am not finished; I shall speak again and again, and I shall raise Mine Voice against them which set foot against Mine servants, and they shall be as ones cast out. So let them ask of Me and I shall enlighten them. So be it I know whereof I speak. Be ye as ones blest to accept Me and know Me for that which I AM.

Sananda

SANANDA

Sori Sori: Let this be Mine time with thee and let it profit thee; and let it profit them which see and read and comprehend that which I say. It is for the good of all that I speak - so let it be, for it is so spoken that they profit thereby.

This I would have them know: There is no other way unto salvation save by Me, the Lord thy God. They think to turn aside and at the last moment rush in?

Nay! I say, they shall be as ones prepared. They shall be first prepared. Then they shall come in and sup with Me and I shall be as the father which receives his wayward son. This is the Word I would give unto them this day.

Sananda

* * * * * * * * * * *

Beloved Ones: This day let it be said that it is now come when there shall be wide spread rumors of peace - and there shall be no peace, for the peace which they ask is but appeasement. They have not found peace, for it is not within them. It hast not been established within them, yet they speak of others as though they had the power to give it or take it away.

I say, let Peace be established within thee, and no man can take it from thee. So be it; I have spoken of peace, yet they have not found peace. I have Peace, yet they have not accepted that which I offer them, for they sit in the seat of the scorner, the bigot, the hypocrite. And they speak of Me and about Me, knowing Me not. I say, they deny Mine sayings, they but mumble that which is accredited unto Me. Yet I say this day that they shall hear that which I say, for I shall shout it from the mountain tops.

I say, first seek ye the Light, and no man shall close it out. I say, no man shall deny thee. Let it be as thou prepare thineself, thou shall receive. So be it, I say. Seek ye the Light and let peace be established within thee, and no man shall take it from thee. So be it.

I AM Sananda

* * * * * * * * * * *

While it is not yet come that they have found peace, let it be said that peace only comes from within. No man finds it from without, for it is his own inheritance and he pilfers not that of another. I say, when they hold subject another or impose upon another that which they have fortuned unto themself, they shall pay, for the law is clearly stated: "Ye shall not trespass upon the will of another." That implies any body of people; that implies the countries, the nations, and the single individuals.

Now, when a plan is established, that each one has his own will granted unto him, he shall be solely responsible for the way in which he goes. Each country, nation, or individual - each shall take upon itself/himself the responsibility for its being, or that which hast been brot into being.

While the nations of the Earth are battling for supremacy, I say, none are sufficient unto themself. Let it be understood that the time draws nigh when the way in which the greatest of all nations has chosen to go shall be cut off - it shall be closed and their progress shall cease. For it is not given unto the Light Forces to be still, without movement - they move with precision, knowing in which direction they go. Let it be said that aggression shall cease, and it shall not be tolerated! For this hast the Great Assembly raised its voice.

Let it be said that the hostilities shall cease - for this have I spoken out. Yet there shall be great conflict ere it ceases. Let it be, for this is the clearing away for peace. I say, they shall learn to love one another and have peace within them. They shall learn from their suffering - so be it the law that they learn. So be it We shall not deny them that. When it is come that they have learned, We shall then give unto them a hand, and it shall be for the good of all, so let it be. I am the One Sent that there be Peace, Light and Love established within them.

So be it I Am One of the Council

* * * * * * * * * * *

Beloved Ones: Hear ye this and know ye that this is the day for which thou hast waited. Let it be said that this is The Day of The Lord, wherein all the prophesies shall be fulfilled - wherein all the Holy Words shall be brot to pass. I say, this is the "Day of full-fill-ment," and for this hast thou waited, yet not in vain.

I say unto thee: The Sacred Writ shall be remembered and it shall be brot to remembrance in the days of fulfillment, for there shall be cause for remembrance. And when it is come that they are brot face to face with their foolishness, they shall be reminded of their folly and the Words which have been given unto them that they might have wisdom. I say, it hast been repeated many times: Look ye unto the Father for thine sustenance and know ye that He is the Giver of Life - He is the Cause of thine being, and He gives and He takes, without revenge. So be it that He hast given unto thee graciously and lovingly - and then I see them turn their face from Him and seek in dark places for wisdom.

Wherein have they found their freedom? Surely, not in the world of men. Wherein have they found peace? Surely, not within the "world of men."

I say, I come not to bring peace, yet I come that they might know from whence cometh their peace. Let it be established within them, and no man can then take it from them. So be it; I have repeated it many times, yet there is no peace within them which cry Peace! Peace! Peace! They but make a mockery of the word, and at no time shall they find it without. They shall establish it within themself, then they shall be as ones prepared for the Greater Part. Let it be.

I AM Sananda

* * * * * * * * * * *

Sanat Kumara speaking: With the Love and Compassion which is Mine, I bow before the Light which I serve - and I place within thine hand Mine hand, that ye might take it - that ye might have Mine assistance - that ye might know that ye walk not alone.

So be it that I am One of the Mighty Council, and at no time shall We betray our trust - neither shall We forget that which has been said unto thee. Let it be said this day that the way is opened for thine return unto thine abiding place. I say, ye shall return unto thine Source and receive thine inheritance in full.

Now, let it be said: Not all shall accept the Gift of comprehension; not all shall accept the Gift which has been given for their acceptance - they have but to prepare themself for to receive it.

It is said, "Cut away thine legirons"; ye cannot bring them into this place, for therein is wisdom. When it is said: "Prepare thineself," it is little understood by man. For to prepare thineself is to be able to receive the Greater part. And it is the law: the Cup shall first be emptied out/cleansed, that it be filled with the First Substance, that of Light Substance - which is the first and pure Substance.

This is the turning away from the old, the putting on the new; the shedding of the old garment, the taking up the new, the bright and shining Armor of God. The Light is not tarnished; it is pure, shining, and dazzling to behold. I say unto thee, place thine hand in Mine - accept that which We offer unto thee, and be ye as one free forever. For this have I revealed Mineself unto thee. Blest are they which know Me, for I am He which is known as,

Sanat Kumara

* * * * * * * * * * *

Beloved of Mine Being: Let this be written for them which will that they might read, that they might know that which I say. Let it be written that they might read, that they might have the knowledge that there is A Plan and that they are not the creators of it. I say, they run hither and yon, asking of man and his opinion that they might find consolation in their own; and it is for this that I speak out at this time. When it is given unto man to know his Source, he shall at no time ask of another his opinion, for he shall have the knowledge of all things what-so-ever. He shall no longer ask of others his opinion about anything, for he shall KNOW and for a surety.

I say: When he hast become unbound, he shall know and be as one wise. Yet it is given unto man as a whole to seek for Light, and he knows not whither to go that he might find it. He hast neither the mind nor the will to search out the Light - to seek out the Light that he finds his way. I say, it is given unto them to weary of the search; they falter near the attainment; they heed not the admonition; "Come." I say, they weary and fall by the way; hear ye that which i say and know ye that there are many prepared to assist, yet they have their hands above thine head.

They are not thine servants - they give unto thee work which shall be done, and at no time shall it be more than ye can bear. They give generously of themself that ye be strengthened in thine weak parts, and that ye be about the Father's business. So be it that I am One which has given of Mineself that ye be spared this day, that ye be as ones prepared - that ye be kept for this day. Now, it is given unto Me to know that which lies before thee and I speak wisely and with compassion.

Let it be written that the time draws nigh when the floods shall rage; the fires shall take many forms, and it shall lay waste the wonderlands of the world. It shall leave behind it the blackness of destruction and desolation; it shall sweep the lands wherein there is great and marvelous forests; it shall be as ye have not seen.

Let it be written that the water shall be of no avail, for the waters shall not be unto them comfort. It, too, shall be as one gone mad; it, too, shall be as ye have not known, for the lakes shall dry, the rivers shall change their course - they shall overflow their banks. The dams shall break, and I say unto thee, they shall be as ones entrapt - distraught - and there shall be great loss of property, and many shall lose their forms of flesh.

Now for this have We said: "Prepare thineself" - fear ye not and seek no hiding place, for there is no hiding place. I say, Seek ye the Light - let peace fill thine heart and know ye that ye are not alone. So be it. I am One which stands by to give assistance; be ye as ones prepared to receive it, for it is proffered in Love and Mercy and with Wisdom. Be ye blest of Mine Presence - I AM thine Older Brother and thine Sibor.

Sanat Kumara

* * * * * * * * * * *

Mine Beloved: The time cometh when thine lands shall bring forth no vegetation, no place where they might turn for relief. While it is said that they have not the comprehension to know, the eyes to see, they have not been unto themself true. For where shall they escape? I say, there is no escape! They shall be inheritors of their desolation, for they shall lay waste the land, and they shall inherit their desolation. So be it and Selah.

Let it be said that they shall cry for relief, and great shall be their torment. So be it that We of The Council have provided a way for the Just and Obedient. I say, the law is just and all who abide thereby shall be called "Just," and they shall be spared the torment which the unjust shall endure. I say, as they have sown so shall they reap - so be it the Law, and the Law is Just. For this is it written that they shall be warned.

Let them which have ears to hear, hear; them which have a mind to learn, let them learn - so be it; I have spoken that they be spared. So let it be - I AM.

* * * * * * * * * * *

Beloved Ones: This is Mine time, and I say unto thee, hold thine head high and be ye as Mine servant. And let not the foul winds blow into thine dwelling place, for I say unto thee: Them which strut themself and they which bear false witness of Mine Servants shall be brot to account for their folly. So be it. I see them running hither and yon and being unto themself great comfort.

I say, they comfort themself, and it is given unto them to be boastful as well as deceitful. So be it that I am come that there be Light; and it is given unto few to stand steadfast and seek the Greater part. They are content to accept the praise and glory of men, yet unto them I say: Be ye not puffed up, for the day cometh when ye shall cry for assistance. So be it I know, for the law is just.

I ask only obedience unto the law - and none maketh a mockery of Mine Words unknown, for all things are known within the place wherein I am. I am not mocked, for I say unto them: The day cometh when I shall go out and I shall walk amongst them as one unknown, and they shall not have the comprehension to know Me. For I am not to be put aside, neither am I to be put into a closet.

I say, there is no hiding the Light which I AM. And too, I say, woe unto any man which deny Me - for I say, I am Sent of Mine Father that there be Light, and for this has He Sent Me. So be it and Selah. I have spoken unto the foolish which think themself wise. So let it be.

Beloved Ones: This day let it be recorded that which shall be given unto them. There shall be a great uprising within the land, and it shall be the fortune of many to be as ones deprived of their vehicles, and they shall be tormented. I say, their torment shall be fortuned unto them thru and by the oppressors and the oppressed, for the two shall come together on one common ground and they shall stand face to face in conflict. And it shall be the beginning of a great struggle for supremacy.

I say, the oppressed shall raise up and they shall be of great strength, for they shall be as ones which have overthrown the law and taken unto themself the authority. They shall take the law into their own hands, and there shall be great and terrible violence. While I say unto thee: It is the beginning of a great conflict - it shall be the beginning and the end, for I say unto thee: Justice shall reign supreme, and for this do ye wait.

Wherein has Justice been supreme? Wherein has Justice reigned? And for this do I say unto thee: Be ye at peace and poise - let not thine tongue betray thee. Be ye silent as the Sphinx and wise as the Serpent. Let it suffice thee that I Am Come that there be Light. So be it there IS LIGHT - be ye one with it. Let no word of hatred or malice escape thine lips - and love ye one another. Be ye blest - for this do I come.

I AM Sananda

* * * * * * * * * * *

Sori Sori: Hast not it been recorded that there shall be opposition? And it shall come within the time which is now come, and it shall be given unto thee to know the opposing forces, for they shall be as ones which have come and gone and the ones which have given unto thee their word of loyalty and fidelity unto the Word. I say, ye shall cut them off, and ye shall be no part of their discord or their dishonor - they shall be as ones cut off. And they shall be as the ones which shall be of the cast-off traitor, they shall have no part of thine reward, neither thine energy or blessing.

I say, I bless not the unjust. I give not Mine Blessing unto the unjust, the wayward. I come that ALL be blest, yet when they do defile Mine Word - turn their face from Me and run after strange gods - I turn Mine face from them and I simply let them be. So be it that I, the Lord thy God, do not condone the actions of the hypocrites and traitors! I am not of a mind to assist them - yet it is said they shall cry for Mine assistance. So be it I have raised Mine Voice against them, and they shall know that I have spoken.

So be it, I AM Sananda

* * * * * * * * * * * *

Beloved Ones: Wherein is it said that there shall be great stress upon the people. I say unto thee, great stress shall be upon them, and they shall know much suffering. Great shall be their loss and great shall be the weeping. Women shall know no rest and men shall carry their own unto burial pyres with heavy hearts - and they shall give unto themself no credit for their part in their suffering; they shall call themself innocent.

Yet I ask thee: "Wherein have they cleansed their hands; wherein have they been as ones without hatred, without blame?" Now, it is come when they shall cry for surcease from their suffering, and they shall lament their lot. So be it that they have been warned; they have the law clearly stated. Many have gone before them that the way be made clear before them, yet hatred and greed is their lot - the pity of it - the hatred which they have, the greed - the pity. Such is the way of the unknowing ones - they cry out for mercy, knowing not to whom they cry. Yet when I speak unto them they hear not, for they have not given unto Me credit for being that which I AM.

They think to tie Mine hands, yet I am not bound by their thinking, their opinions, their own law. I am bound only by Mine own Word. I say, I am bound by Mine word unto thee. I have said, follow ye Me and I shall lead thee out of bondage. It is for Mine love solely that I come unto thee, that they might know that which I say unto thee. Give it unto them, and they shall do with it as they will. So be it; it shall profit them to turn from their hatred and sit down as brothers and drink from the same chalice - bind up their wounds and count the spoils. Let it be said they have much to learn from their loss; let it profit them, for this have i spoken. I AM come that there be Light - so let it be.

I AM Sananda - the Lord God

* * * * * * * * * * *

Beloved Ones: This day let it be written that when one asks of the Father, Light, it shall not be denied him. Yet when he seeks of men he shall become confused, for men are within the realm of men within bondage and they are, too, working in darkness, knowing not. While I say unto thee, there is a Host which stands by to assist when the Word goes forth: "Let there BE LIGHT!" - I say, it goes forth as a mighty thrust and it can not be intercepted by the force of darkness. I say, it <u>Can Not</u> be intercepted by the forces of darkness, for it is direct within its course and straight to its point of direction.

Let it be understood that the way has been made strait, and not one shall be unto the other a fortune, for each is a single Unit, a separate Entity/Being/Individual, and hast free will and at no time shall one depend upon another for his passport into the Inner Temple. I have said that each one is responsible for his own passport into the Inner Temple. While many have been sent to show the way, it is their part to point the way, and the part of each one to heed that which is Law. And let it be said that the dogmas and creeds are man's - not Law, for they have bound themself by their Creeds and Dogmas.

Let it be said that when one sets up an Altar in his name and makes certain laws to suit himself, designed to bind them which follow him, he has indeed portioned out for himself a bitter cup. Now, it is said that Great is the Power of the Word and Great the manifestation thereof. So be it I give unto thee the "Word" and it shall suffice thee. Yet ye shall apply the Law and demand of them adherence unto it.

Let them not defile the Altar which I have set up - let them not contaminate the "Word." Let them not bring forth adulteration, which shall be unto them their sorrow. I say unto them, their sorrow! For to do so is pitiful.

I say, to adulterate or contaminate "The Word" is a pitiful thing indeed. So let it suffice that I have given it unto thee in this manner and it hast been recorded as given, and not one word shall be changed. For this is it given thusly, that it stand as Mine testimony unto them which shall follow after me. So be it and Selah.

I AM Sananda

* * * * * * * * * * *

Beloved Ones: Wherein is it said that there shall be great suffering - is it not so? - and when have they known peace? I say unto thee, they shall have peace. Yet they shall first have peace within their own heart. I say, each shall establish peace within his own heart, and he shall be as one at peace. He shall look unto no man to give it unto him, for it is not within any man's power to establish peace within the heart of another.

The word of comfort, promises unfulfilled, are but poor poultices. Let peace be established within the heart and no man can take it from thee, for it is thine. And it is now come when all their promises and their pacts shall be broken, and they shall see the foolishness of such as they are wont to look for within the world of men. I say, they shall turn unto the Light and therein they shall find peace - and they shall find that they are responsible for that which hast tormented them.

I say: Let Peace be established within them, and no man can take it from them. So be it they shall seek the Light and it shall not be denied them. So be it I have spoken unto them which doth seek peace in the world of men. Wherein have they found peace therein?

Mighty is the Word of the Lord and great the power thereof. And I say unto thee, let peace be established within thee. Let thine own light so shine that all might see it and be drawn unto it.

I AM Sananda

* * * * * * * * * * *

Beloved Ones: While it is the time for rejoicing, I say unto thee: There is great sorrow within the land. The people are sorely oppressed, and they find no rest. I say, they know no peace - yet it is given unto Me to know that which torments them. Too, I know wherein their peace lieth.

I say, they are tormented and know not that which torments them. Let them turn from their own waywardness, their own wanton / selfishness / hatred, and they shall find peace.

I say, peace shall be found within themself, for they shall first establish peace within them, and then they shall bless themself as they would have Me bless them. So be it, I am come that they might know wherein their peace lies.

Bless thine own self by establishing peace within thineself, and no man shall deny thee that gift, for it is thine by Divine right - so accept it in the name of the Father which hast sent Me.

So be it, I AM Sananda

* * * * * * * * * * * *

Blest are thou, O Mine Children, blest art thou - let it be, for this do I come. I speak unto thee from out the inner Temple wherein I abide. I come as one sent, that I might add Mine Blessing. For this have I waited.

This day I would say unto thee: There is a Mighty Host which hast drawn nigh unto the Earth that she be lifted up. So be it that I am one of the Host, and it is given unto Me to see them which walk amongst thee and to know their going and coming - and it is the time for which We have waited, when they might have concourse with the Earth and the people thereof.

It is said that there has been such concourse, and it is no more. I ask, wherein have they been schooled? Wherein have they learned such wisdom as they are so wont to expound? I say that there is the concourse between thee and this place wherein We, the Host, abides, and at no time shall the ones which think themself wise pilfer the Secrets of the Inner Temple. I say, they shall prove themself, and then we shall take note of them. So be it; I am come that they be informed, and that they might come to know that they are not alone. I say, they are not alone, for we have Emissaries amongst them which they know not.

These have not the mind to betray themself - they walk softly and gently amongst the ones which have the mind to usurp the power and authority which is theirs. 1 say, they shall not put their hands into their pockets, for the Emissaries know their weakness (the weakness of the traitors); I say, the ones which would usurp the power and authority of the Emissaries shall learn well their lessons. They shall come to know that there are none so foolish as the ones which think themself wise. So be it, I shall speak unto thee again and again, for I am come that ye might come to know Me. So be it.

I AM One of the Host

* * * * * * * * * * *

Mine Beloved Ones: This day I would say unto thee that Mine Servants are more blest than all the crowned heads of the Earth. I say unto thee: "Mine Servants are more blest than all the crowned heads of Earth," for they shall wear the Crown of Glory - theirs shall be the greater.

So be it that I remember Mine Servants and reward them In like measure for their service. Now, let it be said, no man knoweth the measure of Mine Servant's service, for they have not the greater vision. So be it that I am come that these things be remembered. And no man can measure another's stature by thine own, for to attempt to do so is folly, for thou knowest not thine brother. I say, thou knowest not thineself, for that matter - so be it ye shall come to know. I Am he which knows, for I Am one with Mine Father which hast sent me.

I AM

* * * * * * * * * * *

Beloved Ones: The time is come when ye shall bring forth great fruit, and it shall be good. It shall be of a variety which they have as yet not tasted. I say, they have as yet not tasted of the fruit which ye shall bring forth, and it shall be good, and for this have prepared thee.

Let it be said that I shall raise up Mine Servants, and I shall exalt them over the kings of the Earth, for they shall do greater things then all the kings. They shall be as ones exalted above all others which doth sit in high places of honor - for Mine Servants shall be equal unto Me; for they shall sit upon Mine right hand and they shall bow down unto no man or his puny opinions. They shall know from whence their help cometh, from whence they came and the CAUSE of their Being. So be it; I am come that Mine Servants be lifted up. So be it and Selah.

I AM Sananda

* * * * * * * * * * *

EL-O-HEIM

Soran Speaks of the Candidate

Soran Speaking: While I am One of the Eloheim, I am not of the Earth – I am not of woman born – neither am I of the nether world. I say unto thee, I Am of the ELOHEIM, and I am prepared to speak unto thee thusly:

Be ye as ones prepared to receive that which I say unto thee. When it is given unto one to be lifted up, he has been obedient unto the law which is given unto them (the Candidate). They walk as the initiate; they are not as the "infidel" They betray not themself - they know that there is not any value in the work of the sinister force.

They have their hand out that their fellow man might be lifted up, yet they do not force it upon him. He shows his hand and exposes not himself unto them which would be unto him great torment.

It is now come when it is necessary to walk silently and with dignity, that ye expose not thineself unto the wanton ones. I say, let them seek thee out, and be ye as one prepared to give unto him as he is prepared to receive. Let him seek first the Light, and no man shall take from him his right to see the Light.

Yet he shall prove himself, and he shall find it necessary to walk the way set before him. I say, the Candidate shall first prove himself; then he shall be as one lifted up, for it is given unto him to first prepare himself for the Greater part. So be it and Selah.

Let him which has ears to hear, hear that which I say unto thee and let him profit thereby. I am come that they might be blest of Me and by Me.

I AM Soran

* * * * * * * * * * * *

Soran: Mighty is the Word of God, and great the power thereof. For this let it be said that there is a mighty cry going out from all the Earth and the Word hast gone out: "Let there be Peace! Let there be Peace!" And it shall be brot about thru the ones which are of a mind to follow in the footsteps of the ones sent that it be established upon the Earth.

It is said that there are ones which have given of themself that there be peace. Yet they are not come that they transgress the law, that they trespass upon a people, a nation. They are come that the people be caused to awaken unto their true identity, their inheritance, their own responsibility. And it is said that peace shall be found within them. They shall have no hatred within themself; they shall bear the responsibility given unto them.

Yet I say unto thee: Each shall bear his own responsibility. He shall walk upright, and as one which hast the mind to follow in the footsteps of the "Wayshower." Many have been sent that peace be established within them, yet they have not established it unto themself. This is their own responsibility, their own part. No man can do more than show the way - give them the law and be unto them Brother. I say, they ask not of the Father for peace that they be comforted - they ask of man.

It is as tho they were prepared to accept it; yet they are given a stone when they ask for bread. It is said: "Seek ye the Light, ask of the Father thine freedom," yet they know not the Father, they ask of their idols, their own making. They make of men heroes and give unto them great glory. I say, they are as the ones crying for bread, knowing not from whence it cometh. It is Mine part to give unto thee this Word that they might receive it, and it shall profit them which doth comprehend Mine Word - for this hast it been spoken.

I AM thine Brother of the Inner Temple

* * * * * * * * * * *

Beloved of Mine Being: By the hand of the Almighty Father have I been sent that ye be brot out of bondage, that I might assist in the Great and Divine Plan. I say, it is for the great and mighty assembly that the plan is carried thru, that it be carried to its completion, its fulfillment. I tell thee that the plan is far greater than man hast known, for the fullness hast not been revealed unto him.

He is not as yet prepared to comprehend - for this he has not prepared himself. He hast not as yet overcome the selfish ways which is his; he has within himself that which holds him bound. When it is said: "Cut away thine legirons," he has not comprehended the meaning thereof, for he yet drags them with him. Yet he asks for the fullness of the "Plan," as tho it wast a piece of paper upon which he might behold some sort of magic. I say, the fullness his mind could not grasp; the fullness he could not comprehend, for it is great in scope and perfect in its first magnitude. I say unto thee: Be ye as one prepared to receive it, for art thou not part of the Plan - art thou not part?

I say, behold the work of the Plan; see it work. Be ye one with it and comply with the law set forth, and be ye glad for thine knowing the law, for it is given unto thee to be one which has been given the law, and it shall be fulfilled unto the letter. So be it and Selah.

Now, ye shall remember thine Benefactors and give unto them credit for that which they are, and give unto thineself credit for being a Son of God - for thou art, you know. Has it not been said before? Be ye blest this day - for this have I come forth. Therein is Mine Word unto thee.

I AM

* * * * * * * * * * *

Beloved: This day let it be recorded that which I say unto thee, that they might bear witness of these Mine Words. I AM the Lord God - I AM of mine Father sent that there be light within the world of men. There is light - I say, behold the light which I AM. Let it be known that I AM Come, and as they are prepared so shall they receive of Me. I say, they shall first prepare themself for to receive me, then I shall reveal Mineself unto them. Too, I say, pity are they which deny Me, for poor in spirit are they.

I say unto thee: Behold Me, the Lord thy God, and know ye that thou art not alone. I am come that there be Light, and no man shall keep Mine own from Me. For I come that I might find Mine own, and Mine flock shall hear Mine Voice and answer Me.

When I say unto them: "Come, follow ye Me," they shall lay down their implements of war, their pruning shears, and their titles/their letters/their degrees. They shall throw off the yoke/their mantles/their garments of state, and they shall follow Me as ones glad and joyous, for the Peace which is Mine is that which they have not found within their places of abode.

I say: "Come, follow ye Me, and I shall give unto thee Water more potent than old wine." Pour out thine old wine, and I shall give unto thee living water. So let it be.

I AM Sananda

* * * * * * * * * * *

While it is but a short while until their activities shall be ended, I say, it is now the beginning of the end.

There shall be greater stress before the end, for all their hatred, all their bigotry, all their weakness, shall confront them. They shall be as ones tormented by their own weakness, their foolishness, and their hatreds. For is it not said: "That which they send out shall return unto them, and it shall either bless or torment them"?

It is clearly written: "That which they send forth shall return unto them, as bread upon the water," so shall they eat thereof. And they shall be responsible for that which they have sent out. It is not an unjust law, for it is the law which is and ever shall be - so be it that no man shall set it aside or make it void.

Let it be said that they which bring forth the law of death shall live by the law; they shall be responsible for that which they bring forth. They shall not place their responsibility upon another that they escape the law. Let it be known that when one takes upon himself the responsibility of depriving another his right to express thru the form of flesh, he hast transgressed the law and he alone shall atone for it - none other. Too, it shall be stated here that the ones which stand witness bear testimony of their actions and raise not their voice in protest, are not innocent of guilt; they are likewise accountable for their part.

For I say: To uphold the law of justice is the part of all men which expect justice. Now let it be understood: no man shall take the law into his own hands - he shall not kill. This hast been said many times in many ways, yet they make a mockery of the law and they spit upon the Words which have come forth from Mine own mouth. I say they are willful, and they are to be found wanting.

So be it I shall again this day give unto thee another part for them which shall be added unto this - so let it be. I am with thee that they might know that which I say. Let them take heed, for I say, woe unto them which go headlong unto their downfall. I say unto them: "STOP! LOOK! - see that which ye bring upon thine own self." So be it I say unto thee, Mine Beloved: Return again this day unto this Altar, and I shall speak unto them which are the errant ones.

While it is time now for them to come forth and declare the Truth and be as ones prepared, they shall be given that which is necessary for their preparation - and they shall either choose it or reject it. Yet I say unto them, they prepare themself, none other. They are responsible for their own preparation and they shall find no scape goat which hast the power to do their preparation for them. There is no such law which shall make it possible.

Now, let it be said that they which practice such injustice one unto the other as they are wont to do, shall be unprepared in that day when they shall stand as ones shorn of all their power, all their vain glory - and when they shall be caught up short of their course. So be it that I have given of Mineself that they be prepared to go where I go, yet none enter into Mine place of abode unprepared. So be it that I say again: "Prepare thineself that ye might enter into the Inner Temple with Me" - for this have I come that ye be prepared. So let it be.

What else matters?

So be it, I come that there be light. There is light - see it and walk ye therein.

I AM the Lord thy God, Sananda

* * * * * * * * * * * *

Beloved Ones: This day I would give unto thee this Word - and be it understood that all which ask for Light shall receive. Now, when it is come that ye have made thineself ready for to receive of Me and by Me, I shall reveal Mineself unto thee. Ye need not go into any place; ye need not ask of any man, neither shall ye bow down before any strange god and ask of him favors.

I say, ye shall have no need of thine idols, thine portions, which have been unto thee sedatives/sedations.* Ye have said thine mantrams as rigamaroles, and as poultices they have served thee. While it is now time to be up and about thine Father's business - alert thineself and be self-responsible, responsible for thine own words/deeds/actions. Pilfer the words of no man, for they are his. Make of thine own self a chalice that it might be filled to overflowing that others might fill themselves from the overflow, for there are ones which have a lesser capacity. Fret not for them, for they are content with the droplets from the cascade which abounds endlessly and without ceasing!

Wherein is it written that I shall be the oil in thine lamp? I speak unto thee in parables that ye might know that which is the law, that ye might come to know Me as I AM.

Now, ye shall be as ones prepared to accept the fullness of Me, and I shall not deny thee, for Mine Father and I are One. Hear ye that which I say unto thee: "MINE FATHER AND I ARE ONE" Be ye one with Me and I shall lead thee out of bondage!

* That which has lulled thee to sleep.

I AM that I AM

* * * * * * * * * * *

Blest are they which receive it unto themself - and so shall it be; so shall they be blest of Me, the Lord God, sent of Mine Father that there be light. So be it I Am He which cometh in the night while they sleepeth, knowing not that I Am Come.

I say unto thee, declare unto them I AM COME! Wait upon Me and I shall show thee greater things than they have dreamed of. I say unto them: "Awaken that ye might see the glory of the Lord." Yet they sleep - they grovel for a pittance and wage war upon one another. They spit upon Mine Word, and call themself wise. I say unto them, "COME," and they move not. They have no fear of the darkness, yet they turn from the Light / say, they are the ones which know not. I Am Come that they Know - yet they shall turn from their wanton/willful way and follow after Me.

I come not to show Mine wounds or perform for them miracles that they might follow Me. I give of Mineself that they might know the

Truth which shall free them from bondage. I bring no creed nor dogma - I come solely because of Mine love for them.

I AM the Lord thy God, Sananda

* * * * * * * * * * *

Abortions

When it is come that they bring forth children which are malformed and they deny them and their right to express themself, they are as ones preparing for themself the bitter cup. For I say unto thee: "The procreation act is sacred," and it shall not be given unto them to escape the law when they use it for their own satisfaction, without thot of the results thereof. I say unto them, they are responsible for the results thereof.

When they call for a BEING that he might take upon himself a vehicle of flesh and then they destroy that embryonic vehicle, it is indeed their "bitter cup," for it shall bring about a race of barren women which hast not the power to bring forth and the fortune to be tormented thereby. I say, they shall be tormented because of their inability to bring forth children. These shall be as ones which have not heeded the law of procreation. These shall be the ones which have given of themself in sexual indulgence and <u>self</u>-indulgence without the Light which governs such creation.

Let it be said that there are none exempt of or from the law. The abortions are the undoing of many which are now practicing such, as they are wont to free from responsibility. While it is said that there are none exempt from the law, there are ones which are incapable of bringing forth offspring. These are ones which have fortuned such conditions unto themself in time past, and they, too, are under the law.

Let it be said that they shall suffer the results of such as abortion, and they know not how great their suffering shall be. Such is Mine Word unto thee this day. A word should be sufficient, yet they shall go their way and heed not that which I say. So be it that I see them as a heedless lot - for this have I spoken out that they which have asked might KNOW THE LAW.

So be it, I AM Sananda

* * * * * * * * * * *

Beloved Ones: While it is the time of communicating by this method, this means, I say unto thee: Let this be recorded that others might see and know that there is such communication, and they shall give heed unto that which is recorded - and for this is it given.

When one has been called out from amongst them, they are not of them longer. They say that which is of the Light; they walk upright; they give credit unto the Father for their Being and unto Him credit for the Law which I bring unto thee (the law which no man shall nullify or set aside).

Now, I say unto thee: Wherein is it said that they shall not kill?

Wherein have they transgressed this law?

Wherein have they loved one another?

Wherein have they pilfered the fortune of other nations?

Wherein have they been perfect in the sight of the Great Council?

Wherein have they thought themself wise?

I say unto them, ye bigots! Ye bigots! Plunder no more thine brother's lands - pilfer no more their fortune. Give heed unto Mine Words and let not thine foot slip. For it is now come when the Mighty Council shall take action, and it shall set strait that which hast been made crooked!

I bring with Me a Mighty Host; I bring with Me Power and Authority. I bring with Me mercy and judgement - I KNOW the law and I abide thereby. Yet the law is just, and it is given unto Me to know Mercy. So be it I shall show Mercy in all Mine dealings. Yet I say, they shall cry out against Me; and they shall curse the elements and be as the ones which torment their brothers - and they shall find no place wherein to lay their head. So be it, I say unto thee - be ye no part of them, for they shall be as ones removed into a far corner and they shall no more torment Mine people. I speak unto them which have ears to hear, eyes to see - for none other shall hear or see. I have said: "See ye the hand of God move," for it shall surely move swiftly and perfectly toward the end, which is perfect and in balance according unto the law - the Perfect Law - which I bring.

I am come that there be Light. See it. Behold its action. Be YE ONE WITH IT, AND THERE SHALL BE PEACE.... Sananda speaks of the Law, which IS and EVER SHALL BE, So be it,

I AM HE

* * * * * * * * * * *

Sori Sori: Wherein is it written that ye shall bear witness of Me? Wherein is it said that ye shall follow Me? And is it not lawful? I ask of thee: Wherein hast thou looked for Me, for Peace, for Light? I say unto thee, thou hast wandered far afield, looking afar for Me - for peace - for Light, yet I am not afar off, neither have I been!

It is said: Look neither here nor there, for I AM with you. It is so, so be ye mindful of Me and know ye that I am nearer than thine hand and thine foot. So be it that I Am the Lord of Old - I Am the Lord of Yester-year - I Am the Lord of today - I Am the Lord of tomorrow. I change not - I AM THAT I AM - I come that ye might know Me, that ye might be prepared to go where I go. So let it be.

I AM Sananda

* * * * * * * * * * *

Beloved Ones: This day let it be recorded that all might see that which I say unto thee. There is great stress upon the people of all the lands, and they know not whither to go that they might find peace. Yet it is said that they shall find no peace until it is established within their hearts. They have not established peace within themself. The transgressors are the transgressors still, and yet these are the ones which sit in high places and talk of peace!

I say unto them: They shall obey the Law first and last, then they shall find that others shall find their way unto the council table. First, I have given unto them the Law that they shall abide by: "Thou Shalt Not Kill." They have gone their own way, heeding not the law - yet I say the law is exacting; it IS the Law. They which take up arms against their brother shall perish by their own weapons. So shall it be, for it is the law. Let it be said that when a man speaks of peace, yet he hath no love within his heart for his fellow man, is no indication that peace is established within him, for he fears his enemies - his part, which he has fortuned unto himself.

He hast not known peace, for it is not within him. Let it be said that Peace (?) is the part which they have given unto the poor (?) - the poor in spirit know not peace, for they have not known Me. They deny Me - for this are they poor in spirit. I say, poor are they; they know Me not. Yet they shall call upon Me, saying: "Lord, Lord, give us peace!" while they but make a mockery of Mine Name. I say they know Me not.

So be it, I say unto them: "Be ye accountable unto the law and responsible for thine own actions/words/deeds, then I shall hear thine petitions." So let them which have ears to hear, hear that which I say unto them.

I AM Sananda, the Lord thy God

* * * * * * * * * * *

Soran Speaks of Sananda and Himself

Soran Soran: Holy, Holy is the Word of God. Holy, Pure and simple is His Word. Make ye ready thineself to receive His Word, which shall profit all which shall receive it unto themselves, for He hast given of Himself that they might be lifted up. So be it that ALL which seek the Light shall receive of Him, so let it be. I am come that I might add Mine Light unto His that there be Greater Light within the Earth. I say unto thee: There are ones within thine midst which hast come for that purpose, and it is Mine part to give unto thee this Word.

There are ones which have no knowledge of Me, neither the Lord God or the Father which hast sent us. While they know not, it differs not with us: We come seeking not recognition of men. We come solely because of Our Love and Compassion for them, that they might be brot out of bondage, that they might have freedom as We know freedom. So be it I am One of the Eloheim, and I give of Mine Light, Mine Love, that they might come into the place wherein all Things are known.

So be it that I am He which hast waited long for this part, for this time when the Sons of God shall gather themself together as One Nation and One People, as One Church, as One Mighty Council. And I say unto thee: This is the action for which We work; this is the action taken that there be Peace within the world of men, amongst all men. Yet the Ones which are not responsible for themself shall be removed, and they shall be replaced with the ones which have become responsible.

I say unto them: Be ye as ones responsible for all thine actions, all thine deeds, all thine fortune which thou hast fortuned unto thine own self - so be it the law.

I speak this day that they might know that which I say unto them. So be it that the way is now clear before thee, that ye might come into the place wherein there is no darkness, no mystery, no fear, no danger, no want, no death, no hatred - only Light - and therein is Love, Pure and Holy in its Purity. They shall rejoice and be made glad. So be it and Selah.

I AM Soran

* * * * * * * * * * *

Beloved Ones: While it is yet time, let it be understood that there are many which cry: "Lord! Lord!" yet they know Me not.

I say unto thee, I Am the Lord of Old! I AM THE LORD GOD OF OLD! I Am the Lord God of yesterday, today, and tomorrow. I Am He which is sent of Mine Father that He might Be glorified in Me, thru Me, and by me that the Earth and the Children thereof be lifted up. So be it that I Am the same yesterday, today, and forever. I Am no less for bringing Mineself unto thee - I Am no more for going unto Mine Father, for I AM HE. THE FATHER AND I ARE ONE.

And it is said: "Man, know thineself and ye shall know Me, the Lord thy God." So shall it be, for this do I reveal Mineself at this time. I say, awaken all ye children of the Earth! Awaken all ye nations of the Earth! For it is now come when ye shall be brot to account for thineself! I speak unto thee that it be so - so let it be.

I AM Sananda

* * * * * * * * * * *

Sananda Speaking: It shall be for the benefit of them which seek the Light that I speak unto thee. Let that which I say unto thee be recorded thusly:

There are ones which seek the Light which I AM. There are ones which run after strange gods, and these are the ones which believe Me not. I say, they seek afar, they know not that I Am Come. I say, these are the unknowing ones.

While they know Me not, I say unto thee: Thou knowest Me, and it is fortuned unto thee to follow after Me. So be it that I bid them:

"Follow ye Me," yet they hear not. They ask of men and they put words into Mine mouth which I spit out, for I do not put Mine foot into a hole - I know the pitfalls. I say unto thee, hear ye that which I say, and thou hearest Me. Yet they are deaf; they are as ones prone to bigotry and selfishness, and they think themself wise. They fret for small things; they tear the Light, knowing only the darkness. They hide themself that they might not be known unto Me - they think to deceive Me.

I say, they know me not. While I am come that they might know, they are prone to the learning of books. They pilfer their sayings and speak as the machine and know not the meaning of the words they prattle so freely, that they might be justified in their dealing, in their frailties. I say, they are wont to justify their injustice, their bigotry, their frailties and foolishness. Poor foolish mortals they be.

I say, these shall come to know their frailties, and they shall find no justification in Mine sight. They shall not be Justified by Law, for there is no law which justifies these things - them which betray themself. So be it that I have spoken freely and fearlessly about and unto the bigots, the fools - for it shall be given unto Me to set them strait. So be it i Am Come that they might have Light. So be it, it is the way of the Initiate to give of himself that others be delivered out of bondage. So let it be as the Father hast willed it. I Am He which is Sent that there be Light.

I AM Sananda

* * * * * * * * * * * *

Sori Sori: Has it not been written that this day shall bring forth great stress, great weariness, great learning, great knowledge, and a wayward generation out of which shall come the greatest leaders known unto men? It shall be the "Age of Awakening," and the awakening shall not be painless!

Yet it is given unto Me to see them wandering hither and yon seeking of men, asking for opinions, seeking verifications of their own opinions. Now, these shall find that they are misled, misguided - they have betrayed themself, for they have not sought Truth from the Fountain Head. They have added unto the darkness of ages past their own, and they have become so burdened down with their dogmas and creeds that they can no longer find the Kernels of Wheat which is hidden within the ash. I say the "ash," for it is now come when they shall search the ash for that which is left.

Now, ye shall give this unto them that they might come to know; they shall first seek Truth from the source, and they shall know for a surety. They shall be given as they are capable of receiving. So be it that I know their capacity. While it is given unto Me to be the Lord God, Sent of Mine Father that they be lifted up, I see them as ones willful and wanting. They deny Me - Mine Word - Mine Servants - Mine Messengers - Mine Emissaries.

I tell thee of a surety that these shall come to know that they have betrayed themself; they shall fall by the way bruised, sick of heart, fearful and disillusioned - and then they shall cry out, "Lord! Lord!" and they shall come to know that they have been given a bare bone, that they have found thereon no nourishment, nothing to sustain them in the time of stress - nothing to give unto them freedom from bondage. And as a last resort they shall cry out for their idol; they shall bury their face in their hands and cry aloud for surcease from their grief, for they shall have such as they cannot bear alone. I say, they shall cry out even as the cry of the frightened child. They shall prostrate themself before their empty shrines and cry aloud, "Lord! Lord! hear ye our petitions and give unto us comfort, for we are spent," Then they shall remember that which I have said unto them.

I say unto them: Turn unto the Light - seek ye the Light which I AM, and give unto Me credit for being that which I AM.

When they come unto Me with a contrite heart filled with love and when they are wont to turn from their ways of darkness, I shall receive them unto Mineself and make of them servants. And they shall first accept Me as their own Lord God; and then I shall touch them and they shall know Me as the Son of the Almighty Father which has sent Me.

I AM that I AM, Sananda

* * * * * * * * * * *

Beloved Ones: This day let it be said that the ones which so revile against Me shall come to see that there is no other way in which they enter into the Holy of Holies. I say, I AM the Way, I AM the Door thru which they enter. None enter save thru Me, for I Am the Door - I Am He which is Guardian of the Portal and none enter unknown unto Me.

I AM HE which knows the thots of men; I see their deeds which they are wont to hide from Me. The poor of spirit - these are impoverished and they know Me not.

Let it be recorded that I AM Come that they might come into the place wherein I abide. Yet these poor of spirit know not that I am come - they ask of men? They question of men? They search of the learned; they seek the answers within the pages of history, yet they find no satisfaction. They are not as yet awakened. I say, they have as yet not awakened, for they are as yet asleep!

Let it be said that they, too, shall awaken in due season, and they shall be glad their sleep is past. Let it be said that they shall ripen as the fruit on the vine; then I shall pluck them out, and they shall serve Me and they shall be glad.

So be it that I have spoken, and thou hast heard Me.

I AM Sananda

* * * * * * * * * * *

Soran speaking: Beloved Ones: This day let us consider the great responsibility for the ones which sit in high places. These are responsible for the conduct of themself as well as the ones over which they preside.

Now, it is given unto thine people to call themself free, "A Free People." Wherein have they been free? Wherein have they free speech, freedom of action? I say, they know not freedom! They but think themself free while they are bound by flesh - by the law of gravity - by the attraction of the Moon - by the tides - by man's opinion, his actions - and for the most part, their own legirons! Yea, I say unto them: They know not freedom, yet they shall endure greater bondage 'ere they know the freedom of which I speak.

They have accumulated many legirons - many, many laws have they made for themself which they shall be responsible for. They have not obeyed the Law which was given unto them from the beginning; they have transgressed the first law - this is the pity. While they revile against the ones which transgress the law which they are wont to make and enforce, they have transgressed ALL the Commandments given unto them!

I say unto them: Be ye responsible for that which ye set into motion, and be ye without blemish. Be ye spotless of character. Let thine light so shine that all might honor thee and know that thou art of good character. Be ye not tainted with or by the wonton of fornication, the fornication which is given unto them in high places of thine society.

Be ye clean of hands and be ye pure of thot; let not thine hand be swift to pull down the Standard of the Crown and the Cross. Shall it not be thine deliverance? Be ye swift to uphold Law and Justice - the Law of which I speak. For it is the LAW OF JUSTICE, and no man is to be excluded or exempt for their position or earthly stature. I say, because of position in high places they shall not be exempt. These shall be the beacon lights - these shall be the pillars of government - these shall walk as ones sober - as ones justified, and they shall be beyond reproach, For I say, they shall serve well their fellow man, their brethren, impartially and without malice or prejudice.

I say, these shall be given a part within the Government of the Earth, and therein shall be placed the ones which shall set strait that which hast been made crooked. So be it the hypocrites shall be removed into a corner, and they shall learn well their lesson. For this shall they be given a lesser part. It is said: "Pity is the one which betrays himself or his trust." So it is.

I come that ye might know that which is designed, that which shall come to pass. Yet each and every one shall be responsible for his part within the New Order - I say, none shall shirk his responsibility. So be it that I have spoken unto thee; pass not the Word until thou hast considered well thine own responsibility!

I AM Soran

(This is given at a time when the actions of high-ranking politicians are being questioned.)

* * * * * * * * * * *

Beloved Ones: This day I say unto thee: It is now come when there shall be great stress upon the Peoples of the Earth - yea, and the Earth, for She shall seethe and tear from her stress. She shall tilt and roll - she shall be as a ship tossed about at sea, for she goes thru turbulent waters and she knows no fear. Yet she groans under her burden, for she, too, is ensouled in matter - matter is her cross. She is given unto patience, yet she cries out for deliverance.

Now, when it is come that she goes forth into her new orbit, she shall be free from the suffering and torment which is fortuned unto her now. Wherein is it said, "She shall have a new berth"? [*Prophecies of Other Worlds and The Scripts*] Now, it shall be fortuned unto her to throw off her yoke, and the laggards shall no longer ride her back. I say unto thee: She shall be free of the laggards, and no more shall she given unto them footing. So be it I am come that she too might be assisted in her initiation, in her raising. So let it be, for I AM the Lord God, sent of Mine Father that it be done according unto the Law. So be it and Selah.

I AM Sananda

* * * * * * * * * * *

Beloved Ones: This day let it be understood that service unto one's country is not enough; it is not sufficient unto thine salvation. For to love one another is without counterpart; it is the greatest of all service, service unto thine brother men, men of thine own which are like unto thee. These are thine own kind - yet there is more. Consider well, who is thine brother? Wherein is the other excluded for reason that he has his habitat in a foreign land or that he wears a garment of another color? I say unto thee: "Love ye one another, and thou shall NOT KILL!"

While it is now come that they shall raise up against an unjust system and great persecution, I say unto the oppressed and the down trodden: A new generation shall be raised up which shall go to war no more; they shall bring about a new order, a new system, and war shall be outlawed. So be it according unto the Will of Mine Father which hast sent Me.

I speak out this day as One Sent, that there be Light in the world of men, I say a new generation shall be raised up, and they shall no more go to war. So be it, I have spoken, and I shall speak again and again. I shall raise Mine Voice against the oppressors, and the ones which sit in high places and think themself wise! So be it, I Am the Lord thy God,

Sananda

* * * * * * * * * * *

Beloved: It is Mine part to give unto thee this Word, and it shall be thine part to give it unto them. For it is now come when they shall be tormented by the opposing forces, and there are many, I say unto thee, the opposing force hast no mercy, no ethic, and it is not in any way of that nature. I tell thee of a surety that the opposing forces, which do exist, are of the nether world, and it is not of the Light.

There are ones which have given of themself completely and devotedly that they might destroy that which hast been done within the realms of Light. I tell thee, the time is come when ye shall see the forces of darkness put down - for We of the Mighty Council are not of a mind to stand by and see the Work of our hand devoured by the force which they send forth. We shall move swiftly and silently. We shall give no quarter unto them, for We ask none of them - that is, nothing save obedience unto the Law. This is the time for action! And act we shall! It is Mine part to give unto them the Law, the forewarning, and to carry out the great and divine plan.

Now, I say unto thee: Stand ye steadfast - knowing wherein thou art staid, for I am come that ye know, that ye might be sustained. So let it be for the good of all that I have come unto thee. Be ye blest as I have been blest.

I AM the Lord thy God, Sananda

* * * * * * * * * * *

Holy - Holy is the Word, and great the power thereof - 1 say unto thee: GREAT is the POWER thereof. And Mine Word shall be heard, and it shall bear great fruit, and they shall know that it hast gone forth as a power in the lands of the earth.

The powers of darkness shall not put down Mine Banner, for I shall raise up a people which shall carry it high and uphold its standard. I tell thee of a surety that I am not to be put into a corner - neither am I to be silent - for I see the need of Light in the dark places. I see the darkness go forth as a power which would consume them, were it not possible for us of the Mighty Council to take action. It is by divine command that we do so, and it shall be for the good of all.

There shall be a great clash of powers, and the elements shall do their part. And the waters shall be divided, and the ones which serve Me shall walk upon dry land, dry shod - and they shall know no fear, for they shall know wherein they are staid. So be it I speak unto thee now in symbolic form, that ye might understand that which I say unto thee. The two powers shall be divided in two parts - the Light - the dark. And they shall clash and great shall be the action - and ye shall stand steadfast, knowing that thou art of the Light. And I say unto thee, thine feet shall not be caught in the mire - so be it that I know that which I say unto thee. So let it suffice that I AM the Lord thy God,

Sananda

* * * * * * * * * * *

Sori Sori: This day I would say unto thee: Behold the Work which I shall do. The Work which I shall do shall differ from that of the warmongers, for I shall set up Mine Banner on their battle fields and I shall call from out their ranks men which shall give unto Me credit for being that which I AM.

I shall appoint them Mine guardians of truth and justice, and they shall turn from the wars which men hast fortuned unto themself; and these shall follow Me and keep the Law which I bring. They shall be as Mine Servants, for they shall serve Me with their whole heart and they shall likewise serve their fellow men with Love and Justice for all. I say, I shall recruit from the ranks of men ones which shall be lifted up and these shall never again give unto their brother the bitter cup, for they shall know that they but drink from the same cup. So be it, I have spoken out against the warmongers and oppressors.

Now I say, I shall set strait the way before them, and they which hear Mine Voice shall obey Mine commandment: "COME! COME YE OUT from amongst them and glorify the Father which hast sent Me. So be it that Mine army shall march forth unto a great victory. So be it, I shall lead them, and no man shall lose his life, rather shall he find it.

I AM the Lord thy God, Sananda

* * * * * * * * * * *

Beloved Ones: This day let it be said that there are ones which know not that I am come - while I say unto thee, I Am Come, I AM the One Sent that there be Light, and it is time that they give up their ways of slaughter and hatred and turn unto Me. I tell thee of a surety that their ways shall profit them naught, while Mine Way is the way of deliverance, Peace and Love. It is said: "Love ye one another," yet what do I find? They go into battle as one in royal robes - as ones pure and consumed with a holy purpose.

I say unto thee, their hands are stained with the blood of their fellow men, yea, unto this day they are given unto murdering their Saints, the ones which do crusade for a Holy Cause. They persecute the ones sent as messengers; they run from them and fail to support them and the Holy Cause, while they spend untold amounts on the slaughter of their brothers. Yea I say: "Brothers deny not Mine Word." Know ye that I KNOW that which goes on within the world of men. I tell thee, they are not blameless; they have their hands stained with the blood of their own brothers - for BROTHERS are they! They are from the same root, the same Source - I say, they are from the same root, and they are brothers. Let it be said, they shall answer for their guilt. Let it be recorded that which I have spoken, and they shall come to know that they are the Fools and the Traitors, that they have sold their birthright for a counterfeit quarter, a poor penny.

Now, I say unto them: Ye shall lay down thine arms, and ye shall take up the Cross and follow Me. Ye shall be responsible for thine every act and ye shall atone for all thine deeds - yea, even unto the last. Ye shall be as ones free when thou hast atoned for all thine misused energy. So be it and Selah.

**I AM Sananda, The Lord God,
Sent of Mine Father, Solen Aum Solen**

* * * * * * * * * * *

Behold! Behold the Glory of the Lord! I say unto thee: Behold the Glory of the Lord, and know ye that the time is now come when ye shall see the Work which I shall do, for I shall show Mine hand. I shall do a Mighty Work and no man shall stay Mine hand, for it shall pass over them as a Mighty Power, and that power is not to be pilfered or nullified. I say, the Power of which I speak shall not be pilfered or nullified, for it shall be as nothing seen by man. I say, they shall bow down and seek the light which I AM, for they shall come to know that they are not self-sufficient, sufficient unto themself.

They shall cry for the help of the Power from and of the Mighty Host. They shall bow low, as ones prostrate before their King. They shall plead for help, for they shall be betrayed by father, by son, by brother, sister, mother, and by the friends. I say, these are the days spoken of, of old, as the "End Times," the End Time which shall bring great divisions of all people. And they shall run riot, and they shall be as the beasts of the field.

They shall eat as the beasts; they shall sleep as the beasts, for many shall have no place wherein to lay their head, no place wherein to rest their weary feet. So be it that I have spoken unto thee that ye might know wherein thou art staid. So be it that I Am Come that there be Light - so let it be.

I AM Sananda

* * * * * * * * * * *

Sanat Kumara Speaks

Beloved of Mine Being: Hast it not been said that it is given unto Me to be the Lord of Venus? It is so - yet I am no less for having taken unto Mineself the custodianship of the Earth - for long have I gathered her into Mine bosom. I have watched her thru many perilous times, and I have taken responsibility for her safety. Now it is come when shall reel and roll as a ship, storm-tossed at sea. Yet I say unto thee she shall survive! For this have I given of Mineself that it be so.

Now wherein is it said that: "She shall be given a new berth". It is now prepared within the roadways of the heavens. The way hast been cleared that she might have a port wherein she might be renewed and have surcease from her groanings. She shall no longer be tormented by that which hast been fortuned unto here by and thru the laggards. She shall be free of them, for they shall be put into yet another place wherein they shall first learn the responsibility of their own deeds.

There shall be a resting period for the Earth, for long hast she groaned under her burden. Yet she hast done her part grandly, and Victory shall be here reward. So be it I give unto thee this Word that they might have it at this time, for it is the time of great anxiety and change. Changes is good, and it behooves Me to remind thee of the changes, for there is no stagnation within the Realms of Light. So be ye as ones prepared to go forth to meet such changes with a glad heart. Let it be as the Father Wills it, for art thou not of the "First Born"? So be it and Selah.

I am Sanat Kumara

* * * * * * * * * * *

Beloved Ones: Let it be understood this day that I am the One sent that there be Light within the realm of darkness, for I say, it is thru and by the Light which I AM, that the world of man shall come out of darkness, out of its bondage, out of the pit.

Now, it is accredited unto Me as being the "Savior" of the world. While it is so, it is not fully understood that each and every one hast his own responsibility for himself and his actions. Each and every one has the responsibility or preparing himself for the new day, the day of revelation, wherein he might be as one responsible for the new revelation, the power and the authority which goes with such revelations as I bring.

Now, it shall be given unto each one which chooses Mine Way to have the power and the authority which is Mine, for they shall be equal unto Me in Mine Father's Kingdom. They shall be Co-Creators with Him and He shall give unto them the power and the authority which is like unto Mine, for therein is no inequality, there is not preference, no favor shown. Each shall choose freely his work, his part, which shall be according unto the Great and Divine Plan; and none shall oppose it, for all shall be of one mind, one part, one mind – that of serving the while for the good of all.

Now, when it is said that there are many within the Mighty Host, it is so. And yet they are not divided amongst themselves; they have no thot other than to serve the whole of the plan. The Plan is the fulfilling of the part which hast been given unto thee from the beginning. It is the way which hast been designed for man, which enables him to find his way home – yea to make his ascent from out the pit.

I say unto thee: Man hast created his own pit and hast fallen into it headlong. I Am Come that he be delivered out – yet he shall will it so. So be it he shall first be obedient unto the law which I bring; he shall make ready himself to receive Me, and then I shall give unto him as he is prepared to receive. So be it I do not betray Mineself or Mine trust. I Am come that there be Light.

I AM Sananda

* * * * * * * * * * * *

Beloved Ones: This day let it be recorded that which I say unto thee. It is the time of going and coming, the time of haste and waste. Yet it is given unto some to go out seeking wisdom, and others go for yet another purpose.

Now I say unto thee: The ones which come unto thee seeking wisdom shall be blest; the ones seeking wonders shall not see the work of Mine hand, for the Glory thereof shall be hidden from them. The ones which come seeking [light] shall find, and it shall be their reward. So let them which come asking offal, shall take it away with them, for they shall in no way contaminate thee. Give unto them nothing which they can pilfer or use against thee, for they are the bigots and hypocrites. So be ye no part of them. Let them go their way and give unto them naught! So be it that I have spoken, and thou hast heard Me.

I AM Sananda

* * * * * * * * * * *

Beloved Ones: This day let us speak of "Zeal," the zeal which consumes them, the zeal which gives unto them no rest. This is the misspent energy which is fortuned unto so many. This is the misdirected energy which is so often the fortune of the "zealot." Zealots are prone to the work of bringing others into the place wherein they have not yet entered. The zealot has as yet not drunken the last drop of his own portion, yet he is wont to give it unto his neighbor that he might sup with him.

It is said: "First apply the portion unto thine own self, and when thou hast proven its worth and found the cup sweet, pass it unto thine brother." First prepare thineself, and then thou shall go fetch thine brother, for by thine light shall he follow thee.

Wherein is it said: "Let thine own light so shine that they might see it and be drawn unto it". Yet the blind seeth not. While the blind shall have their eyes made to see, so be it that I shall touch them which are so prepared to receive Me and of Me. So be it and Selah. I am come that they might see, yet there are ones which have not asked of Me. They seek of men, their opinions, and they ask not of the Father for Light. I say, they which ask of the Father shall not be denied. So be it I am sent that there be Light - so let it be.

I AM Sananda

* * * * * * * * * * *

Beloved of Mine Being: I say unto thee this day that once there was a Prophet great of stature, filled with love and wisdom, which knew his Source. And he wast given unto wandering; he wandered the lands of the earth as he awaited the coming of the Lord of Hosts. He carried with him neither purse or food, he called no place home. He had within his hand the power to create for himself the food sufficient unto his need. He called all men Brother.

He carried no penny, no clothing. He wandered empty-handed, yet he did not want. While I say he did not want, I tell thee his waiting wast long and hard. He knew not the hour, the day, the year of the coming of the Blessed Lord of Hosts. He cried out in his longing as tho his heart would break! I say unto thee, weary not of thine lot, for I say unto thee, the waiting shall bring its reward. Hasten ye not to betray thineself, for I say unto thee the waiting shall bring a great reward.

So be it, I know, for I Am He, The Wanderer. I bless thee with Mine Presence. I go as I come and I bid thee, Adieu.

* * * * * * * * * * *

The Wanderer

Beloved of Mine Being: Let this day be a day of great joy, for the time is come when the Mighty Host hast drawn nigh unto the Earth, and it is fortuned unto Me to be one of them. I tell thee, it is a great day and one in which it is come that all the Host be prepared to go forth as to battle, for within the Host there are no laggards.

We of the Host of which I speak are prepared to do battle against the forces of darkness. We are not wanting, for We are well qualified for our part - for this have we prepared ourself.

Not a plan goes astray. We know the plan and are one with it. It behooves us to know and we are not unaware of the forces which beset the World of men. Yet it is of their own making, and they shall be responsible for that which they have created. While it is a sad lot that they are - and their plight is a sad one indeed - they shall be as ones responsible for it. They shall learn well their lesson, which is self-responsibility. They shall learn that they have the power to create either for weal or woe, and that is no small gift.

Let it be said that there is a way unto their Salvation, their deliverance from bondage. It is clearly written that there IS LIGHT, and they have but to seek it and turn from their own puny way, the way which hast led them into the pit.

While it is given unto us to see and to know that which goes on within their secret chambers, I tell thee of a truth: We dare not trespass upon their free will until they cross the threshold of despair, whereupon they shall be stopt! I say, there they shall be stopt!! Know ye this: There are none so sad as the one which betrays himself or his trust, for he is indeed the Traitor. Be ye no part of him; give unto him no footing. Let him go his way and hasten ye not after him, for he shall bring about his own end. Hear ye that which I say unto thee, and be ye as ones blest of Me and by Me. come as one of the Great Assembly, as one which sees the need, and I have answered it. So be it I stand with outstretched hand, extended that all whosoever will might take it, and I shall give of Mineself that he be lifted up. So be it, I Am known as The Wanderer.

* * * * * * * * * * *

Beloved Ones: Mine hand I give unto thee this day. Accept it in the Name of Mine Father which hast sent Me. I say unto thee, the time swiftly approaches when there shall be great rivers run within the deserts, and the mountains shall give unto them no hiding place. They shall flee their abiding places to find no resting place.

So be it that I am come to give unto them of Mine Love, Mine Wisdom, Mine Knowledge, Mine foresight - yet they turn aside and hear Me not. They are filled with fear. They seek safety within their own realm - while I say there is no safety within their realm, for their realm shall be shaken unto its very foundation and they shall run hither and yon seeking peace, and there shall be no peace. For Peace hast not been established within them - they know not from whence cometh their peace; they know me not.

Wherein is it said: I Am thine Shield and thine Buckler, so be it and let it be - for this have I come.

I AM Sananda

* * * * * * * * * * *

O Holy Father, Father of Mine Being - Giver of Life art Thou, O Father, this day I would that they, these thine children, knew thee as i do. Let it be, for this have I revealed Mineself.

Father, Blessed Art Thou, Holy Art Thou, and Mighty is Thine Works. Perfect art thine works.

Keep these Thine Children in the Way Thou would that they go. Hold them, Father - I ask it for their sake.

Thou knowest them and their every need, yet I speak that they might bear witness of Mine Love which I bear for them. For their sake have I bared Mine Cross. For their sake have I gone out from Thee as man. For their sake have I lowered Mine Light, that they might see that which they are capable of comprehending.

Give unto them greater capacity for knowledge, O Father. Let them arise with Me and return unto their rightful estate, that which Thou hast Willed unto them.

Thank Thee, O Blessed Father, that Thou hast heard Me. I bless them with Mine Presence, So let it be.

I AM thine Son, Sananda

* * * * * * * * * * * *

Beloved of Mine Being: Hear ye that which I say unto thee, and know ye that I am come that ye be blest of Me and by Me. For this do I come.

While it is given unto thee to receive Me, it is for the good of all that I speak - and unto all I say: It is good that there be a change in the governments of the Earth. For long hast man-made laws held subject the peoples thereof. Now, it is time that freedom ring out in its true aspect. It shall ring out and the sound shall reverberate thruout the Lands of the Earth. And at no time shall it be an unwelcome sound, for it shall be the call unto freedom. And they which are not held in bondage shall raise up in one accord and they shall Sing Freedom's Song. They shall go forth as one, in one accord, and as one man in this new day. And there shall be no oppressors, for the oppressors shall be put down.

Let it be; for this hast the cry gone out: "LET FREEDOM RING OUT! LET EVERY MAN GO FREE." Yet it is said: "Freedom is Mine, sayeth the Lord God of Hosts, and at no time shall it be required of thee to kill thine fellow man or hold him subject unto thee." I say, he, too, shall be free, and at no time shall ye hold thine own self responsible for his actions. Yet ye shall be responsible for thine own. Ye shall take full responsibility for thine own self - thine every act, or word, or thot. For it is now come when ye shall garner in all that thou hast sown, for it is the reaping time, likewise the sowing, for the seasons are continuous.

Let it be said that there is Light. Walk ye in it. I come that ye might see it. Let it be.

I AM Sanat Kumara

* * * * * * * * * * * *

Beloved Ones: This day let us speak of fear, fear being that which comes from the reason thou knowest not the Plan. The plan is fashioned for the good of all. Yet when one is given over to fear of any kind, it is for the unknowing, the darkness which prevails upon the Earth, that mist which man hast created for himself - the "fog-mist" which shall be put aside when they have asked for Light. I say, when they have asked for Light, the mist shall disappear and be no more. So be it that they are filled with fear; they fear that which they comprehend not. They fear the Light, for they have fortuned unto themself great darkness. Therefore, they are more comfortable within their own environment. They fear being removed from the environment which they have fortuned unto themself.

They have no desire to reach up unto the greater heights. They hope by some miracle that it shall become their fortune to be taken up, up into the realms wherein they might find peace. Yet it is said many times: "Seek ye the Light which I AM and follow ye Me, and I shall lead thee gently into the place wherein there is Peace." So be it, I AM the Wayshower. lam sent of Mine Father that ye might KNOW, that ye might return unto Him with Me - so let it be as He hast Willed it.

I say unto them which fear "Come! Come, follow ye Me and I shall show thee the way unto the Father's place of abode. Fear not." For this have I come that ye be delivered up. I AM the Door thru which thou enter into the Holy of Holies. So be if I AM the Lord of Lords, The Host of Hosts.

I AM Sananda

* * * * * * * * * * *

Hear Ye! Hear ye that which I say, for it is now come when the Word shall go forth which shall call all men to the front. I say, all men shall be called to go forth that this day might bring forth fruit of a new kind.

I, too, say that this day shall be as none other, for it is the day for which they have waited. Now, they shall go forth as warriors anew, warriors for the Mighty Cause, for Truth, Light and Justice. These shall stand as upon the Rock.

They shall not be moved, for it is come when the call hast gone out: "Surrender up thineself and give unto Me thine whole heart, thine will, thine life, for it is Mine." I have given of Mineself that ye have life. So be it I AM the "SOL," I AM HE which hast ENSOULED thee within my being and I ask of thee: Be ye as one with me and ye shall go forward into battle with thine whole armor of light, which none shall take from thee.

I say: Ye shall hold high the Lamp of Truth and Justice, and no man shall put thee down or tread upon thee. I say, stand ye high among men and resist them not, for they are but the ones which shall go down into defeat. For no man shall stand against the Warriors of Light. Hear ye Mine words, for I have sent forth a Fiat which shall protect them which carry the Banner of Truth and Justice.

So be it I speak unto thee as thine Father Eternal - such am I.

And I AM thine Father, Solen Aum Solen

* * * * * * * * * * *

Holy, Holy is the Name of Solen Aum Solen. Peace be unto thee this day, for I say unto thee the time is now come when the hour hast struck, when ye shall see and know the power of the "WORD." Holy, Holy is the Word; see the power thereof, and use it for the glory of the Father which hast sent Me. See ye the Word made manifest and create ye no thorns for thine brow. I say unto thee: "Create no thorns for thine brow" - so be it I come that there be Light. So, let it be.

I AM Sananda

* * * * * * * * * * *

Beloved of Mine Being: Hast it not been said that this is the time of gathering in? And it is so. It is given uno Me to be one of the Great and Mighty Council, and I know wherein they are. And it is given unto us of The Council to be as Ones prepared to go forth that this day be the beginning of a New Order.

I say, that this day be the beginning of a new order, and it shall be as none man hast known, for it shall be the Order of the New Day, wherein all men shall sit down at the Council Table as Brothers. And they shall be as Brothers of ONE ORDER wherein they shall love one another and be as the One which has the peace which surpasses all that which man hast ever known.

For I say unto thee: The New Day shall bring great changes in the complexion of the affairs of men, for there shall be Great Ones raised up amongst them which shall know the Law and they shall be within the Law to govern the affairs of the Government. And for this shall they be given great power, for they shall be sent, even as I AM sent, that the plan be fulfilled - that the day bring forth the fulfillment of the Scriptures.

I say unto them which hast fortuned unto themselves the part of interpreting the Scriptures: Be ye not so sure that thou art so wise, for thou hast blundered mightily in thine interpretation of the records handed down thru the ages past. Thou hast changed the words to suit thine own way, thine own wont. I say, as it hast suited man he hast put upon the Sacred Writ his interpretation. He hast bled white the crimson rose. He hast taken from the salt its savor - and if the salt hast lost its savor, wherein shall it be salt? Such is Mine preachment for this hour, and I am wont to speak on this subject again and again. So be it I shall - for this do ye now wait.

I bless thee with Mine Presence, with Mine Being.

I AM Sanat Kumara

* * * * * * * * * * *

Beloved of Mine Being: Say unto them this day that it is now come when they shall turn from their old way in which they have gone; and they shall now turn their face homeward, for the End Time is now come when they shall no more wander upon the Earth as ones in bondage. The way is opened for their return. Yet they shall choose their way, and it is given unto Me to see them following after strange gods while I am crying unto them: "Come, follow ye Me." They hear not Mine cries, yet they follow blindly the ones which come in Mine Name, declaring falsely that they are from afar, that they are the deliverers!!

I say unto them: These are the false ones which cry out. They are sent for the purpose of distracting thee from the truth, from the Light. They say unto thee: Look there, look afar, and behold what is doing there, while thou hast held within thine own hand the key to thine own salvation, thine own preparation for the Greater part. These are the enemies of the Truth - these are the adversaries - these are the false ones. And I shall point them out, and they shall be known for that which they are, for Justice shall prevail.

I say unto thee: Be ye about thine own affairs, that of preparing thineself for the Greater learning, the fulfilling of the Law. Live ye this day and be ye not fearful for thine life, for thine life is not of a moment. It is Eternal, and great is the work of The Almighty Father which hast sent Me.

I say unto thee: Place thine hand on Mine and I shall lead thee out of bondage - yet none shall bring thee against thine will. So be it I Am the One Sent that there be Light. I speak unto thee as One of the Mighty Council, for I Am the head of the council which is and shall ever be, Worlds without end.

I AM Sananda

* * * * * * * * * * *

Beloved Ones: This day let it be known that I, the Lord thy God, hast come - come unto thee, come that ye be made glad, come that ye be prepared to return unto the Father with Me. It behooves Me to say unto them which seek the Light, which I AM, that they shall not be denied. Yet I, too, say that they shall be prepared to receive Me and of Me, and it is clearly and wisely stated that:" As they are prepared, so shall they receive." It is the Law.

I tell thee, it is now come when they shall cry out for Light and I shall hear their cries, and they shall be given as they are prepared to receive. It is said many times, yet they weary of Mine Word, Mine Counseling, and they look for strange gods and miracles - for this have they been fortuned great sorrow.

They are now asking: Where is He which cometh? Where is He, the Man of many miracles? They want to see the marks upon the body -

they ask for proof!! Yea, Mine Beloved, I say unto thee, they ask that they put their fingers into the wounds. Yet I say, never again shall 1 bare Mine wounds unto them, for they are no more. No more do I carry Mine marks upon Mine body, for Mine is not of Earth. Mine is the body of Light Substance. Yet I can take upon Mineself the flesh as it suits Mine purpose. I am the Master of the Elements, and I know the way of the Elements and too, I know the weakness of flesh.

I say unto thee: There is power in the Word, and I know that power and I use it wisely that Mine Father be glorified - so let it be. Be ye blest this day. I have spoken that it be so, so let it be.

I AM Sananda

* * * * * * * * * * *

Beloved Ones: This day let us speak of Patience. I say unto thee: It is not afar off when all knees shall bend and every head shall be bowed. Yet it is given unto man to be a rebellious lot. It is not the way of man to humble himself before the Great and Mighty Power which is the Cause of his Being. He is wont to forget the Source of his BEing; he is prone to forgetfulness. Yet he shall be brot to remembrance; he shall be caused to remember.

Now, it is the way of the Initiate to stand by in readiness to assist him when he has prepared himself to receive the assistance of the "Initiate." The Initiate is one which knows the way back unto his place of abode from whence he hast gone out. He hast earned his passport into the Holy of Holies. He hast been as one prepared to render assistance anywhere at any time, to anyone so prepared to receive such assistance, for he knows the Law and he does not violate it.

He walks with circumspection and prudence, he wearies not of his waiting. He is at all times mindful of his part which is part of the Great and Grand Plan, and he is in no way of a mind to betray himself or his trust. He is wont to become one with the Mighty Plan, for he knows the Way of the initiate, and he is at all times concerned with the Greater Part. Trivialities are none of his fortune, for he hast the knowledge of all that it fortunes unto man.

He gives not of himself unto gaming - he hast seen the results thereof. The time is now come when many shall give themself over to such as the so-called "Sports," and they shall devote their energies unto this as an occupation. For their sake let it be said that it is the way of the dragon, "Drag-ON," for it is the long way 'round.

I say: It is the poor fortune of man, for I say unto him: "There are more profitable things to occupy thine time and consume thine energy." So be it thine Guardians simply wait, that ye might learn well thine lessons. And it shall behoove the young men to turn to the plowshares and be as the plowmen, for I say it is now come when the fields shall be deserted and they shall yield up no harvest.

And the wind shall blow and the dust shall cover the land and the water shall be as the dirt. Wherein is it said that there shall be great suffering? Yet there shall come a season when the rains shall come and the waters shall cover the land and the men shall be no more seen upon the land, and they shall know that the End Time is upon them. So be it that I have spoken wisely and prudently, that they might be as ones alert and turn unto the ways of the knowing ones and be as one with them that these things might not need be. For it is the way of mankind to hasten the coming events by his own deeds. The deeds and thots are as the sprouts upon which shall grow the thorns which shall tear his own flesh, yea, even unto the very bone!

I speak that they might be spared. I say unto thee, be ye no part of their wanton ways. Be ye no part of their willfulness. Be ye not fearful, for I am come that ye might come to know the way of the Initiate that ye might walk in the way in which I have gone. I say unto thee: "Come, follow ye Me, and I shall lead thee out before the day of Great Suffering." I Am the Lord thy God sent that ye might know.

So be it, I AM Sananda

* * * * * * * * * * *

Beloved of Mine Being: Be ye blest to receive Me this day, for I give of Mineself that ye might be blest. Now it is come when there shall be a glad cry go forth, and it shall reverberate around the Earth. I say, it shall reverberate around the Earth!! And there shall be great rejoicing and many shall fall upon their knees in gratitude, while others shall quickly forget that which hast been unto them great blessing. They shall turn unto their plowing and sowing and unto their places of merry-making in forgetfulness, for this is the way of man.

Let it be said that there shall be great Light shed upon the peoples of the Earth and great shall be their revelations, for it is now come when they which seek the Light shall find it, for it shall not be hidden. I speak unto thee that they might bear witness of that which I say unto thee.

So be it, I AM Sananda

* * * * * * * * * * *

Behold this day the Work which I, the Lord God shall do. Behold the Way of The Lord thy God, and be ye blest. Walk ye in the way of The Lord and know ye that it is the way of Light, the Light which never fails. I say unto thee, be ye blest this day, for this do I speak unto thee. Let thine hand be Mine hand, thine words Mine Words; and let thine time be Mine time, and I shall abide with thee. So be it, I give of Mineself that ye be blest, so let it be.

I AM Sananda

* * * * * * * * * * *

Solen Aum Solen

O, Holy art Thou Mine Son, Mine Son which I have named Sananda by Divine Right. He, Mine Son, cometh unto Me as Mine First Born. I give unto Him the Name from the beginning of His sojourn upon the Planet Earth. I give it Him in remembrance. I speak of Mine Son as the "First Born," for is He not?

I say unto thee: He, Mine Son, the One I have given the name Sananda, hast now come unto Me on thine behalf, that He might have greater, yet greater concourse with thee that ye might be as ones prepared to enter into His place of abode. I ask of thee nothing save obedience unto the Law, and walk ye after Him - Him which I have sent unto thee that ye might return unto Me with Him, Mine Son, Sananda. I speak unto thee in His Presence that ye might bear witness of Mine Word. I tell thee as He would that the Order of Melchizedek be fortuned thine Service which is as none other at this time. For this have I called thee and thou hast answered, "Here Am I." I have not denied thee; I have not cut thee off from Mineself. I bid thee enter into the Holy of Holies and partake of Mine Substance, O Holy Ones of Israel. Walk ye after Him, Mine Son, Sananda, and pass into the Inner Temple as Ones Purified and Justified.

I AM Solen Aum Solen

* * * * * * * * * * *

Behold in Me the Light - Behold in Me the Way, and give unto Me credit for knowing that which I say unto thee, for I am come that ye, too, know even as I know, so let it be.

Rest thine head upon Mine breast and give ye a gladsome prayer that it is now come when ye shall walk with Me, and ye shall know Me as I AM and none shall deceive thee. I say unto thee, none shall deceive thee, for it is given unto thee to know me, and none other shall be as I Am. Yet many shall mimic Me, and many shall come, declaring that they come in Mine Name. Yet I say unto thee, I am come unto thee that ye might know the true from the false. So let them which ask of the dead, have their gods and their guides. Yet ye shall not counsel with the dead or ask of strange gods miracles. So be it I am sufficient unto all thine needs. I am come that ye be lifted up - so be it.

I AM Sananda

* * * * * * * * * * *

Beloved Ones: Who amongst thee is qualified to be unto Me Sibor? Who amongst thee is prepared to lift thee up? Who amongst thee is prepared to give unto thee passport into the place of Mine Abode? Who amongst thee has qualified for the part which is Mine by Divine Right?

I say unto thee: I am the door thru which ye enter into the Inner Temple. I say unto thee, I am come that ye be lifted up. So be it that I come solely for Mine Love for thee, for it is Love which hast sent Me forth as One qualified for the part which is Mine.

So be it that I AM qualified to say unto thee: "Come, follow ye Me and I shall lead thee into the place wherein Mine Father abides." So be it that He hast sent Me that it Be, and no man shall deny Me Mine inheritance, for it is Mine by Divine Right. And at no time shall Mine inheritance be pilfered or dissipated, for it is given unto Me to be true unto Mineself and Mine trust. So all is well with Me. Canst thou say as much? Let it be so, for this do I speak unto thee thusly, that it be so.

While I say there are many which know Me not, they shall come to know ere they pass the portal of Light into the Inner Temple. Hold ye no illusions, for I speak unto thee that ye know the true from the false - so be it that I am come that ye know.

So be it that there are many which shall have a long and troubled sleep ere they awaken. Yet it is given unto the sleeper to awaken in due season - for this do I now cry out: "AWAKEN! AWAKEN!" and all the Nations shall hear in due season.

While the peoples of the Earth shall spill blood of their brothers, they shall overrun the lands (the black hordes) and they shall stamp the soil upon which they tread with their signs. They shall call themself "Righteous" and call their wars "Holy." Holy? I ask: Holy? Wherein have they purified themself? Wherein have they loved their fellow men? Wherein have they qualified themself to sit in judgement? Wherein have they been ordained of Me, the Lord of Lords, the Host of Hosts, the Lord God, sent that there be Light? I say unto thee: They desecrate the Earth, they pillage the poor! They are wont to give heed unto Mine Word, the Law which I give unto them. Yet the Law is not Mine. It is given unto Me to bring unto the Earth - that Law which is that by which they shall attain unto the Greater part (their Eternal Freedom). I say unto them: Be ye not deceived, for no man enters into the Inner Temple save by Me.

So be it I Am the Host of Hosts, Lord of Lords, Sibor of Sibors, the Lord God sent of Mine Father, which hast given of Himself that ye might have everlasting life, so let it be.

I AM Sananda

* * * * * * * * * * *

Beloved Ones: While it is yet time, let it be understood that there is a mighty force abroad within the land, and it is such as would consume them which have not the comprehension of the Light which is, which has always been and always shall be. Yet these which have set this force into action know not the Light, for they are of the darkness and the Light is not within them. They serve the darkness, they generate the darkness - and for that matter, they fear the Light. They fear that which they do not know.

For [because) they are aware of the soil upon which they put their feet, they know that they have footing upon the Earth, while they desecrate it by the willful way which is theirs by choice. I say they have free will to choose which way they go, yet they have sold their birthright for a poor penny, and they have given over their freedom unto them which would hold them bound in darkness. I say unto them, arise, claim thine Sonship, and be ye as ones responsible for thine own self, and know ye that there is Light, The Light which faileth not. So be it that I AM the Light - I AM the Way. Come ye, follow ye Me - walk ye in the Light and be ye as one free from all bondage forever.

I AM the Lord thy God, Sananda

* * * * * * * * * * *

For this day let us consider the "WORD," and it is for the good of all that we take unto ourself this consideration,

When The Word goes out of Mine mouth, it is designed to benefit all beings everywhere! And for this is the Word sent forth. Yet we know that all shall not receive it unto themselves, for all are not as yet prepared to drink of Mine cup. They have not prepared themself for to receive Me or of Me.

I say unto them: "AWAKEN! Arise and prepare thineself that I might come in and sup with thee." Yet they weary of Mine words. They hear not that which I say. They ask not for Mine way - they choose the easy way. Easy? I ask of them: Easy? Wherein hast the way of bondage been easy? I ask of them obedience unto the Law while they tarry in the streets of despair. They sing the song of the desolate, the forlorn, the hopeless. They despair of their lot, yet they have not the strength of character to walk in the way which I go. They despair of the way in which I lead them. I say unto them: "Come! follow ye Me," and they tire of the upward climb, of the preparation. Yet they grovel within the places of darkness for a poor penny - a pittance indeed!!

While I say unto them: "Let them which have a mind come, take up Mine Cross and follow Me." They weary of the discipline which it entails, for I say unto them, the way of the Initiate is thru self-dedication and discipline. And none attain unto the heights until they have learned well discipline, for it is the First Law - that of obedience unto the Law. For the Law never fails; it is impartial and exact in its action, and none invalidate it.

Such is Mine Word this day. Let it be given unto them which have a mind to receive it. So be it Mine hand is upon thee - I bless thee that they be blest, so let it be.

I AM Sananda

* * * * * * * * * * *

The Order of Melchizedek

Beloved Ones: Mine hand is upon thee this day, and I give unto thee this Word that all be blest thereby. It is said that the Order of Melchizedek is not of the Earth. It is so and it is now come when the Earth shall become a greater part of the Order, for it is thru and by this Order, which is the Mighty Council, that this Great Work of purifying the Earth and making it a habitable place for the Sons of God, shall come about. It hast been said: "The Sons of God shall inherit the Earth." It is so - yet she shall be purged, cleansed, and she shall be as one made new. For that matter she, too, shall come into her own thru and by the efforts of the Mighty Council, and it is given unto her now to be going thru great change and great stress.

We of the Council work without ceasing that the Earth and the Children thereof be lifted up, and we are not limited unto the Earth in our activity. Ours is a work of Love, of long duration and infinite in scope. So be it ye shall come to know the fullness of our activity, the fullness of which no man knows until he has won his freedom from bondage.

I speak unto thee of The Order of Melchizedek that ye might come to know thine oneness with it - that thou art one with it, of it. And for this have I spoken unto thee of this in this manner, for it behooves Me to give unto thee this Word at this time, for I see the wisdom thereof and for this shall ye be blest.

I AM the Lord thy God, Sananda

* * * * * * * * * * *

Behold the hand of God - see it move - and know ye that it moves in ways beyond the comprehension of men. For it is the power of the Almighty God, The Father, which shall sweep away all the unsightly, unholy places, and that which hast accumulated therein. I say: It is the power of The Almighty God which shall cleanse the Earth and bring her into the place of her new berth. So be it that it shall be accomplished and she shall be spared! I say, she shall be spared!! So be it according unto the Law.

I Am Come that the Law be fulfilled, that the Scriptures be fulfilled. And at no time shall I deny Mine Love, Mine Service unto the Earth, or the Children thereof. Yet it is given unto Me to know the sorrow and the groaning of these which deny Me. And as for the Earth, She hast cried long for deliverance, and she hast fulfilled her part of the Plan. She hast been the resting place of the sleepers and the footstool of the laggards. Now, she shall throw them off and be as one free of her burden. So be it I speak unto thee of that which is now in progress. So be it that the lands of the Earth shall be overrun with the "black hordes" before the Earth is delivered out. Yet i say unto thee: The end is in sight, and I KNOW, so let it be. For it shall end in a Great Victory for the Earth, which hast received thee unto herself as the place wherein thou hast learned many lessons and wherein thine Victory is won.

So be if I speak unto thee - so let it be for the good of all.

I AM Sananda

* * * * * * * * * * *

Mine Children: Behold Me in all things. See ye the life of Mine Being I have endowed unto all Mine creation. I have created wisely, and I have given unto Mine Creation power to create like unto its kind. Yet I have set man apart, as a part separate from all other, for I have endowed unto him FREE WILL and a part which hast not been given unto the lesser of Mine Creation.

This Gift sets him apart and above his lesser brothers. Yet I say unto thee, the lesser brothers are none the less dear unto Me for they, too, shall find their rightful place wherein they shall know peace. For they, too, shall come into their own realm wherein they shall bring forth greater manifestation and wherein they shall be given a new part. They shall come to have new forms of a finer density, of greater light density, and they shall bring forth greater intelligent beings, creatures of great intelligence such as man hast not seen. And man shall wonder at these creatures of great beauty and intelligence. Yet it is given unto man to be the Guardian of these lesser brothers, the Guardians which have the fortune to be born with the precious, precious gift of free will. So be it thou are entrusted with these creatures which, too, have their place. So be it thou are no less for being their Guardians while they, too, shall be lifted up. Theirs is no small part, for they, too, are part of the Plan within the great Plan. So be it I have spoken and thou hast heard Me.

I AM thine Father, Solen Aum Solen

* * * * * * * * * * *

Beloved Ones: Wherein is it said that the way is now made clear before thee - it is so - and no man shall deny thee entrance into the place wherein l abide. Yet I say unto thee, see and know ye that there is but one Lord of Hosts, Lord of Lords, Sibor of Sibors, and none shall be unto Me a puny pretender. For I say unto thee, The Father hast given unto Me the place, the name and the part which is Mine. And yet I say, there are ones which would rob Me and Mine inheritance, and it is given unto Me to know them - I KNOW THEM! I say unto thee, it behooves thee to be alert and wise, for no man taketh away that which is given unto thee - yet he but waits for thine door to open unto him. He would deprive thee thine right of speech, thine action, thine inheritance. I tell thee it behooves thee to know them. I, too, tell thee, ye shall know them by their fruit. Such is Mine Word unto thee this day - so let it be known that I am with thee.

I AM Sananda

* * * * * * * * * * *

Hear ye this day the Word of the Lord thy God, and be ye as ones prepared for the things to come. Know ye that the way is open before thee - yet there are many which would beset thee which would turn thee from thine appointed course. Know ye that the time is now at hand when the door shall be closed upon them which are weak of character and trail of spirit. I say unto thee, it is now come when the door stands ajar for the strong of Spirit. And the wanton shall not find the latch, for it shall be hidden from the unjust and the imprudent. is it not said: "Ye shall seek the Light with thine Whole Heart, and nothing shall hide it from thee"?

It is now come when ye shall stand firm as the rock, the Rock I have given unto thee. The Rock, The Foundation upon which I have builded, I have given unto thee. Now, ye shall be as the material of which I shall build Greater Mansions. I shall build even greater and no man shall tear down or destroy Mine handwork, for it shall endure. It shall not be vainly used, neither shall the unjust look upon the Work of Mine hand, for it shall be hidden from their sight.

While I say unto thee: Look, See and know ye that I Am Come, that the Kingdom of Mine Father be established upon the Earth. I Am come that ye might see and know, so let it be.

I AM Sananda

* * * * * * * * * * *

Behold the Work which I shall do, for it shall be a Mighty Work which shall glorify Mine Father which hast sent Me. I say unto thee: Behold! see that which / shall do, for I shall touch thee and thine eye shall be opened, and ye shall behold the Glory of the Lord. Ye shall stand in wonderment and ye shall praise the Name of Solen Aum Solen which hast sent Me.

So be it I am come with the Rod and with the Crown. I come with power, with the Authority which is Mine by Divine right. I come unto thee as the First Born, The King of Kings, The Son of God, "The Wayshower." I come unto thee as one prepared to give unto thee as I have received. I come as One qualified to deliver thee out of bondage. So be it that I Am the Lord thy God, and there is but one Lord God. So be it many shall mimic Me and come declaring they are thine deliverer, and they shall be so bold as to use Mine Name.

Mine Words shall they pilfer that they might deceive the unknowing ones. So be it that I am not to be mocked, for these which come declaring falsely shall be exposed for that which they are. And I say unto thee, be ye as one blest to know the true from the false - for this have I revealed unto thee Mine precepts, and I have given unto thee that which shall suffice. Let no man deceive thee, for I am come that ye might know the truth. So be it and Selah.

I AM Sananda

* * * * * * * * * * *

Beloved Ones: This day let it be known that I Am Come, Come into the Earth as man. While I Am not as man, I Am that which is the Master - I am the "Wayshower"; I have overcome flesh. I Am that I choose to be, for I Am one with the all, the Eternal Father. I know Mineself to be one with Him, for I have not separated Mineself from Him. I know Mineself for the which I AM.

I go not, neither do I come - I AM. Yet it is said: "I come unto thee" - so be it, for I surely give unto thee of Mineself that ye might be lifted up, that ye might know that which is hidden. I say, I reveal Mineself unto thee for the purpose of bringing mankind out of their bondage, out of their darkness. Let it be said that I reveal not Mineself unto the unjust and the imprudent. Yet they shall see that which I shall do, for I shall do a wondrous Work. And they shall marvel and mumble among themself at the Work which I shall do, for I shall set free Mine People - I shall cut loose the part which hast held them captive.

I shall give unto the lowly a voice that they might have a voice in the governments of the lands - and I shall be as the one to put within their mouth the words to say which shall astound the wise. For I say unto thee this day, the ones which sit in high places and think themself wise shall be confounded by that which shall be done, for I shall do the mighty Work which shall confound them. I shall bring about a new order among the people.

I shall set up a government for the people in which they shall be free of bondage and I shall pluck out from among the people the ones to be unto Me Mine hands, Mine feet. I shall give unto them the power and the authority to act as Mine Ambassadors; I shall give unto them the words to say, and they shall be true unto their trust. To thee I would say this day: Thine part is no small part, yet thine work hast but begun. Let it be known that which I have said unto thee, and at no time shall ye be censured for thine part.

Let them which have a mind to learn of Me come, and I shall give unto them as they are prepared to receive.

So be it I AM the Lord thy God, Sananda

* * * * * * * * * * * *

Mine Children: Upon Mine High Holy Mountain I view the ways of men - I see and know them, for I Am the Lord thy God. I know them for that which they are; I know them for that which they shall become, for I see the end as the beginning. I say unto thee: The ones I see are varied and many - they are as ones looking afar for that which is ever present, that which is within their hand. They give unto others power to give and to take that which is theirs - they are wont to see that which is before them. They ask of man his blessing when he hast the Eternal Verities within his hand. He hast the power which is his to use when he hast become of age, when he hast learned well his lesson that he might use such power for the good of all.

Let it be understood that appearance is the Great Deceiver, the whore. I say unto thee, be ye not deceived by appearance, for it is but the outer, and no man seeth that which is hidden from the eyes of the unjust and the imprudent. Listen unto Me, O ye children! Know ye that it is now come when ye shall sit with Me in Council, and ye shall be as ones blest this day. And I say unto thee, let thine own Light so shine that all might see it and follow it that they might know that thou knowest Me, The Lord thy God.

Sananda

* * * * * * * * * * *

Hold ye the Light - know ye that there IS Light. Walk ye therein and ask of no man that he be unto thee servant, for I say unto thee: Man is a poor servant, for I, the Lord thy God, knoweth thine needs - thine every need. So be it I give unto thee that which thou art prepared to receive, that which shall profit thee. So be it that I bless thee with Mine Being - with Mine Own Hand have I blest thee. Now I have said unto thee: Thou shall bless others as I have blest thee.

So be it that I AM Sananda

* * * * * * * * * * *

Beloved Ones: Mine time is come and I say unto thee: Many come in Mine name wherein they proclaim great, wondrous words, powers. Miracles do they perform that they might astound them which know not the false from the true.

I say, they which know not bow down and worship the false and the magician, while I stand by and wait for them to learn well their lessons. Then they shall have the comprehension which is required of the Initiate. I say, the Initiate seeks nothing save Truth - Light and this is that which shall be revealed unto them which seek Light,

Let it be said that Light is Justice; Light is the Power thru which they shall be delivered up. I say, the Power which is the Life, the Way - is that which shall deliver them up. They shall find that no man is responsible for them. No man is their Master which taketh upon himself their load, their responsibilities, their frailties.

They shall learn that they alone are responsible for their weakness, and they shall learn well that they have no "Scape-goat." They shall become the age of responsibility; they shall be as ones responsible for all their misused energy, for it is said, and rightly so: There is no such law of "Vicarious Atonement!" No such law hast been given unto man. For this do I say unto man: "Awaken! Be ye as one responsible for thine own misused energy. Turn from thine own and seek ye the Light." This I have said many times, yet they look afar for a Savior, an easy way.

I say unto them, obey ye the Law, apply it unto thineself, and be ye diligent in its application and ye shall be thine own savior in the doing. Hold high the Lamp which I have given. Drink ye from Mine Chalice, and I shall give of Mineself that ye be lifted up. Ye shall do thine part, and I shall not forsake thee in the time of trial. I bid thee, awaken, arise, come, and be ye as ones prepared to enter into Mine place of abode.

                                                        I AM Sananda

* * * * * * * * * * *

Beloved Ones: This day I say unto thee: There are none which have the power to stay Mine hand, for I, the Lord thy God, shall do a Mighty Work, and they shall see that which I shall do. While they know Me not, they shall see the work of Mine hand, and I shall set strait that which hast been made crooked. So be it that I, the Lord thy God, hast the power and the authority, the wisdom to bring them out of bondage. While they cry unknowingly that I am come, they cry out for deliverance, I hear them and i shall find them which cry unto Me.

For 1 say they are Mine People, Mine Flock which are downtrodden and suppressed by the ones which have set themself up, them which sit in high places and call themselves wise. Let them be, for they shall be brot low; they shall fall and be as ones broken; while Mine people shall arise as on wings of the morning, and they shall no more know war. They shall no more know suppression, for they shall be delivered out. I say, I shall find them and I shall deliver them out. So be it I am come that it be so. So let it be.

                                                        I AM Sananda

* * * * * * * * * * *

This day let it be recorded that which I say unto thee, and it shall profit all which have a mind to follow in Mine footsteps. It is for this that I say unto thee: Be ye as ones prepared for the GREATER PART. I tell thee this day, it is the Greater Part for which thou hast waited. Thou hast as yet not tasted of the greater part, for flesh cannot endure that which is kept for thee; flesh is the weaker/lesser part. While the Spirit has not lessened by coming forth as the flesh - that of coming into flesh/matter - Spirit is no less for being the person. While it is not the person, the personality - the personality is superficial and not the REALITY. The personality is that which is cultivated and which is come into being from and thru experience, while individuality is yet another subject, which I shall speak of at another time for which ye shall wait. So be it that I shall wait for that part. Let it be.

I AM Sananda

* * * * * * * * * * *

Sori Sori: Let this be recorded that they might know that which is said unto thee. Behold the hand of God move; see it move and know ye that I am the Lord thy God. So be it that I am aware of the Sons of God, their places, their parts. I am aware of the Traitors and their parts which they play with such audacity, with great and pious pomp. They are wont to be given instruction from and by the forces of Light; they betray themself. They are not as the Sons of God; they are not of Mine Flock, for I am not of them. I give not Mineself that they be strengthened - I give not Mine Cup unto them that they sup with Me.

I withhold Mine Cup from them, for they do make a mockery of Mine Words; they sell their heritage for a poor penny. And at no time shall I betray Mine trust or Mineself, for I am come that there be Light, so let it be. Let them which have the mind to follow Me, come, and these I shall counsel. These I shall lift up and these | shall bless, for I am come that they might be found, sorted out and prepared, that they might enter into the Holy of Holies with Me.

For it is now come when many shall be brot out, and they shall be given a new body, a new place of abode; and they shall know that I AM and that they have at last found their way into Mine place of abode. I say, it is the way of the Initiate to walk with surety, and as gentle as the fallen dew shall he go amongst them which know him not. For he, the Initiate, shall not flaunt himself, neither shall he reveal himself unto the uninitiated, for he shall be as silent as the Sphinx. He walks softly and silently amongst the unlearned. He hast at all times, the authority and the power to assist the one which hast the Will to follow Me - he knows the true from the false. So be it, I speak unto them which have ears to hear and a mind to learn.

So be it, I AM Sananda

* * * * * * * * * * *

Beloved Ones: There is a plan, a time of fulfillment - and the joy of that fulfillment no man knows. So be it that I see the joy of its completion, for I see it as done. And the time swiftly approaches when it shall be given unto thee to see as I see. So be ye not anxious for that which is yet to come; wait upon Me, The Lord thy God. Give unto Me credit for knowing that which I say unto thee.

Fear not that for which thou hast not yet seen, that which is to be. Be ye blest this day and give unto thineself peace. Let it be established within thee; be ye at peace and poise. Seek not the fortune of the magician, for they are not of Mine Flock, for I give unto thee that which is sufficient unto thine salvation.

I say: There are magicians which give unto them that which they seek, yet it is not the ultimate; it is not that which bringeth unto them Eternal freedom. I am come that thine bondage be ended, that thine eternal freedom be thine this day. So be it I say: "Follow ye Me" - yet they weary of Mine Sayings and they turn unto the magicians that they might see his miracles! That they might see his miracles, that they might be given the miracles of flesh - the signs and wonders which doth astound them. So be it that they are astounded by that which he does; for this do they follow him, the wonder-maker, the magician.

I say: I come not to astound them, neither to bewilder them. I come that they might come into the fullness of their inheritance. So be it I give unto them that which is sufficient unto their salvation - yet they have as yet not given unto Me credit for being that which I AM.

I say unto them which ask of Me: "Come! Follow ye Me and I shall counsel thee, and I shall lead thee out of bondage forever." So let it be, for I come not preaching a strange or new doctrine. I simply give unto thee the Law which is as of old, that which shall be unto thee thine passport into the place wherein I AM. I ask of thee nothing save obedience unto these, and therein is thine own freedom. So be ye as one self-responsible - I am come that it be So.

I AM Sananda

* * * * * * * * * * * *

Beloved Ones: There is but One God, One Lord God, One Mighty and High Council - "ONE," And none other shall ye serve, for I say unto thee: There are ones which set up their own altars, and they build great and wondrous temples unto their strange and powerful gods which hold them bound. They give unto these "gods" the power to hold them, for they pay homage unto them. They perform magical rites unto them; they ask of them favors, signs and wonders, knowing not that by these they are bound unto their strange gods.

They have not learned that they bind themself unto these strange and false gods. They are wont to give unto Me credit for being that which I AM, yet they give unto these the power to deceive them by their magical rites. They have not learned that they alone give unto these the power to hold them within their grasp. These are the ones which seek signs and wonders, knowing not that these are the tools with which the magician can bind them.

I say, be ye alert - hold high Mine Lamp, that which I have given unto thee. Walk ye not with them which would mislead, for they but give unto thee the bitter cup. I say: Be ye as ones blest to hear that which I say unto thee, and I shall be unto thee sufficient unto the day. Rest not on thine Laurels, for there is yet Greater things in store for thee. Be ye as ones alert. Let no man trip thee up, for it is now come when the dragon shall be brot out into the open, and he shall be exposed for that which he is!

I say: Ye shall know him for that which he is. He shall have no power over thee while thou art with Me, for I have said unto thee: "I Am thine Shield and thine Buckler." So it is; IT IS SO! For I am not a traitor - yet I say unto thee, turn not thine face from Me.

Keep thine eyes fixed upon the Way in which I lead thee, for I shall lead thee aright. Fall not unto The Tempter, for he shall do a work which is designed to tempt all men to follow him. Be ye as ones forewarned of his Magic. Believe him not, for he is a liar, and the truth is not within him - I come that ye know the true from the false.

I AM Sananda

* * * * * * * * * * *

Beloved Ones: Let this be given unto them which have ears to hear that which I say, for I say it that they too might know that I am come for the good of all - for the GOOD OF ALL! Let them, too, know as thou knowest.

So be it that there is a movement abroad in the Lands of the Earth to give unto all men freedom, and this is not a small or insignificant thing. Yet I say, man hast not the power to set them free, for the forces of darkness hast so woven their web that they, the people, hast no power of their own, for they have surrendered up their will. They are possessed; they are as ones filled with hatred. Now, this is not of the forces of Light - I say, they have given of themself, their energy, unto the forces of darkness. Now it is come when Great Light shall be upon all the peoples of the Earth and there shall be great unrest, for the darkness shall be brot out of cover/uncovered, and they shall know wherein they have been bound. They shall see the folly of serving the forces of darkness. They shall seek the Light and it shall not be denied them, for when they turn from the darkness they shall face the Light. I say unto them which have wearied of the darkness: "Turn ye, follow ye Me and I shall lead thee into the place wherein l abide. COME! and be ye free, even as I am free."

I AM the Lord thy God, Sananda

* * * * * * * * * * *

Beloved Ones: This day let it be recorded that which I say unto thee. The time draws nigh when the mighty hord es shall roam the streets as ones gone mad. They shall pillage and burn the places wherein they have been, as the offenders shall they be; they shall be as ones obsessed, and at no time shall they be given one iota of assistance from or thru the Mighty Council. These hordes shall strive to put down the law by which they have prospered, or by which they have benefited. I say, they are not respecters of the law. They shall give of themself that the law be put asunder, that it be broken - and the pity of it: they, too, shall be broken! They, too, shall be put down. So be it that these are the ones which have not heard that which I say - these are not of a mind to follow after Me. I say unto thee, they have set into motion that which shall be their own undoing.

They shall be as ones gathered together, and as sticks they shall be broken - broken by twos and threes, yea, by fours shall they be broken. Yet there are the oppressors. These, too, shall be broken as a reed upon a rock. I say, they shall see the frailty of their own strength, for it shall fail them in that day - the day of Judgement. Hear ye that which I say unto thee: It shall fail them in the day of Judgement. So be it I know, yet I am not the judge - I Am the One Sent that there be Light, so let it be.

I AM Sananda

* * * * * * * * * * * *

Beloved Ones: Be ye at peace - peace I give unto thee; let thine time be Mine time. Rest in the knowing that I am thine Shield and thine Buckler, and at no time shall I deceive thee. I hold thee within Mine embrace, and I shall not let thee go. I am come that ye might have communion with Me, that ye might know Me, that ye might be as one with Me. I Am the One Sent that ye be found and brot out of bondage, for long hast thou been bound in darkness. Now ye shall wait upon Me, the Lord thy God, and no other gods shall ye have before Me. Such is Mine Word unto thee this day.

So be it that I AM Sananda

* * * * * * * * * * *

Beloved Ones: The time arrives swiftly when there shall be great black hordes roaming the streets and crying for blood, for it is the fortune of them which have been bound within flesh to be as ones bound - bound by the dragon, oppressed by him - and they have held out their hand unto him. He hast licked it; now he shall bite it, for he hast no scruples. He hast no ethic; he is the deceiver and the purveyor of lies. He hast not the Grace of the Lord thy God; he is the one bound in perdition. He hast not the will to let go the oppressed - he hast the will to hold them bound. Now, I say unto thee: Hold ye steadfast and turn not from the Light. Fear not and grovel not unto the ones which sit in high places. So be it, I am with thee unto the end.

I AM Sananda

* * * * * * * * * * *

Beloved of Mine Being: This is Mine time to speak out, for I am silenced for long and at no time shall I break Mine silence for naught. I say, it is now come when I shall speak out against the aggressor, against the ones which hold in bondage the oppressed. I say, these which hold in bondage the oppressed are the oppressors, and they shall be as ones responsible for their own deeds of oppression and aggression!!

I say that the aggression is that which hast been unto Me the stench in Mine nostrils, for I say it is the aggression which is the downfall of many a nation and people. They think to prosper by their aggression and pillage/plunder - hold sway over the lesser nation. They fall victim into their own weakness; they fall into the pit which they have prepared for their brother. Let it be said that they which set the trap for their brother shall be bound therein; I tell thee of a surety - they shall not prosper! For it is the Will of The Father that all men be free. Yet no man shall take upon himself the burden of another man's wrongdoings. He shall be as one responsible for his <u>own</u> actions, his deeds, his own "Sins." Let it be known now that each hast the responsibility of his own wrongdoing, his own aggression, and none shall find where the law justifies him for his aggression.

I say unto them: Be ye as the keepers of the law - take not the law into thine own hands, to thine own end, for thine own benefit! I say, it shall profit them not; for that matter, it shall be their own undoing. So be it I have spoken out and I am not finished, for I shall speak again and again. For that is Mine part that the Way be made clear for the ones which have asked of Me that they be delivered up that they might have the opportunity to gain their own freedom from bondage. Let them which have ears to hear, hear that which I say. So be it, it shall profit them, for this have I spoken.

I AM the Lord thy God, Sananda

* * * * * * * * * * *

Beloved Ones: It is now come when there shall be great rumblings within the Earth, as tho the winds blow within her. There shall be great rumblings and groanings from within her, and it shall cause great tidal waves such as thou hast not known. Yet I say, it is given unto man to bring about his own downfall, for he hast not obeyed the Law - "LAW" - the Law set forth from the beginning. I say, the Law by which he shall live ere his deliverance from bondage.

Now let it be said: I am not the Law Giver. I am the proclaimer of the Law of which I speak. I am the One Sent that they might have the Law by which they shall live ere they are delivered out.

So be it that they shall bring about their own downfall by their own disobedience unto it, their disrespect for the Divine Law set forth by The Father, Solen Aum Solen. So be it I say unto them: "LOOK! SEE! Behold ye the Hand of God; see it move and be ye as ones awakened from thine lethargy, I COME THAT YE AWAKEN.

I AM Sananda

* * * * * * * * * * *

Beloved Ones: While it is yet time for thine preparation, it is given unto thee to be as ones with the vehicles of flesh, and for this do ye come under the law of flesh. I say, each hast its laws, laws for each and every place of abode, even as for each and every household. Each a law, for each hast its Head and each hast its Feet - each hast a place within the whole of society. "So above, so below," for it is the Greater Household to which thou belongest - it is Mine and I Am the Head of this household and thou art Mine feet, Mine hands, Mine Servants.

So be ye as ones prepared within the place wherein thou art, that ye might come into the Inner Temple with Me and rejoice for thine preparation. So be it I am with thee. I am not afar off - so be it that I Am The Lord Thy God.

Sananda

* * * * * * * * * * *

Holy! Holy! is the Name of Solen Aum Solen. Speak it with reverence and remembrance, for He hast given unto thee Life - LIFE OF HIS LIFE - and now it is thine time to remember that which thou art. So be it I shall touch thee and ye shall remember. So be it I Am the Lord thy God.

Sananda

* * * * * * * * * * *

Beloved Ones: While I say unto thee, the Spirit is that which motivates the flesh, that flesh comes under the law of flesh. Yet the Spirit is free from the law of flesh, and the flesh is bound by the law of flesh, while Spirit is not bound by any law of flesh nor Earth. The flesh is weak, perishable, while Spirit is imperishable and cannot be contained in flesh. Spirit animates, uses, and holds for a time an instrument of certain form, color, size - releases it, and then takes upon itself another, and yet another - according unto its need, its desire, its likeness. Wherein is it said: "From Glory unto Glory"?

Wherein is it said: "From the heights hast Spirit descended into the depth, and unto the heights shall it return unscathed, unharmed for its descent." Let it be known that Spirit speaketh unto Spirit, for flesh comprehendeth not that which Spirit sayeth.

So be it that I AM THAT I AM, Sananda

* * * * * * * * * * *

Beloved Ones: This day let it be said that thine Mother Eternal hast nourished thee and held thee unto Her bosom in the time of thine long sojourn within the realms of manifestation. For it is by Me, for Mine part, that thou hast been comforted, fed and nourished while thou hast been within the manifested realms. While it is said that "ye shall return unto thine rightful estate," I say, ye shall no longer be bound in the denser world of the denser forms, the manifest world - that which is seen and felt by flesh.

WE are thine Eternal Parent, not Parents. We are ONE with our creation, our manifestation, for thou hast come out of Mine womb, nursed at Mine breast - YET NOT AS FLESH. While it is given unto thee to have the parent of flesh, so dost thou have Mother of Spirit, for flesh is the counterfeit, or counterpart of Spirit - Spirit, "So above, So below." While the Spirit is but the great Animator of flesh, flesh animates not. Flesh is weak, and Spirit is free. So be it that flesh comprehends not the things of Spirit.

While Spirit knows the weakness of flesh, it is the Animator, and the Greater. In no way shall Spirit be less than Spirit, and that which IS shall always BE, while flesh shall pass unto its Source, that of the chemical world, the elements from which it is taken. So be ye as ones prepared to step forth as ones free from thine "pore" of chemical substance, and be ye as ones free forevermore as ones glorified, free from bondage of flesh - of the manifest substance of the world of dense form. There are forms, myriads of forms more glorious than thou hast imaged which is not of chemical substance. Let the mind which is Mine be the mind which is thine, and I shall sustain thee. I shall be unto thee all that thou hast need of, for I AM thine Mother Eternal.

* * * * * * * * * * *

Sori Sori: So it becomes necessary to give unto them this Word, and it gives no comfort unto the unjust and the imprudent.

It is given unto the Mighty Council to sit in Council for the benefit of all mankind, yet not all know that We exist, or that we are at the Father's Business. We are not amiss; we are not intruders in the affairs of men. We trespass not upon the free will of man - that is, without he dare go so far as to jeopardize the whole.

It is for this that I say, We sit in council for the good of all. While no man knows the extent of our work, he hast not the mind to comprehend the fullness of it. Yet We sleep not, neither are we in lethargy - We are alert as to the Power of the Spoken Word, the power which is given unto the Spoken Word. Yet we are alert unto the frailties of mankind. We know his blunderings and his progress; yet he hast not learned the power of The Word.

For he spews from his mouth words of profanity and words of hatred, and he gives unto it power which goes out as a great dark, black cloud, dense and stench! And he hast given unto these words of hatred and profanity power! And it hast taken form, and that form shall be as a great Black Dragon which shall turn upon him and devour him - swallow him up! And he shall perish by his own creation!

I say: It is now expedient to speak of these which have created such as that which now beclouds the Earth. It is of man's making, for the Father hast not created such fiendish schemes. There is no such law as they have been wont to set into motion. It is said: "Thou shall not KILL!" Wherein hast the Father given unto them to take that which they cannot give? It is the downfall of many generations/civilizations - and again I say unto them: "Be ye mindful of that which ye set into motion, for it shall return unto thee, prest down and running over. Be ye as ones responsible for thine actions; walk ye circumspect in all thine ways, all thine days, and bless thineself in the doing." So be it I have spoken of the transgression of the Law, and there is no Justice therein.

So be it I say unto thee: Give of thineself that peace be established in the world of men, and ye shall be as one which knows peace, and no man shall take it from thee.

So be it I have spoken, and it shall profit thee to heed Mine Words, for this have I spoken them. Blest be the ones which heed that which I say unto them.

         I AM the Lord God, Sananda

     * * * * * * * * * * *

Beloved of Mine Being: It is now come when they which have set themself up as the Mighty Council which was designed to rule all men and which was designed to be the force of the Nations combined, shall be given little or no credit. It shall be flaunted; it shall be as the many treaties which have been of no value in keeping the Peace, for it shall be as naught. For man hast not peace within him. Man hast not as yet learned the first lesson: "Love Ye One Another" - and for this shall all their instruments of peace fail until they have first established peace within their hearts. Then no man shall take it from them, for it shall be the Peace which is Mine. I have said: "Mine Peace I give unto thee," yet they have not as yet accepted it.

So be it there shall be much talk of peace, yet they go headlong into war! What kind of peace is this? I ask of thee! See that which they do and that which they say, and know ye from whence cometh their suffering and torment. Yet ye shall be no part of them, for they set themself apart from Mine Flock by that which they do. I say: "By their fruit shall ye know them."

So be it I have spoken as One of The Great and Mighty Council - I Am the Head of that council.

So be it I AM Sananda

* * * * * * * * * * *

Behold the Power of God, O Ye Mighty Sons of God. I say unto thee, behold the Power of God - look not unto men! LOOK! SEE! Behold the Hand of God move, for it is the power by which Sons of God are born! It is the power by which the crooked shall be made strait; it is the Power by which all things are brot forth from out the Light Substance. I say unto thee, behold ye the Light which I AM.

Behold the Light which thou art; know ye that the soul winds shall not bring unto thee the stench from which they have emanated. I say, the stench is offensive unto Me, for Mine Words have been used for their own willfulness, their own cause.

Their cause is not Mine. They have been as the "Judas," for they have sold their part for a poor coin which shall burn their fingers. Let them be - be ye no part of them, and be ye as one at peace. Know ye that: "That which hast been made crooked shall be made strait." So be it and Selah - for this do I speak out this day. For this have I revealed Mineself unto thee. Be ye at peace, poise, and know ye that the Hand of God is swift unto Justice.

I AM the Lord thy God, Sananda

* * * * * * * * * * *

Behold ye the Work which I do, for I AM the door. I AM that I AM, and thou shalt have no other God before Me. I say unto thee: Thou shalt have no other Gods before Me. Wait upon Me and I shall do a Mighty Work, for I Am the Giver and the Taker - I Am The ALL. - and I am no less for having parts, for thine body is but part of the whole of Me. For this have I said: "Thou art Mine hands, Mine feet, made manifest upon Mine Earth".

Mine is the Earth and millions, yea, ten thousand times ten thousand million worlds, and I have peopled them. I have created after Mine own imaging. I have imaged Mine creation, and they are like unto Mine; they are formed after Mine plan, for I say unto thee, there is a plan. Be ye as ones prepared to see the fullness thereof and know ye that I AM thine Eternal Father, from which thou hast gone forth from Me.

Now I say unto thee: "I shall bring thee back unto Me as the extension of Mineself, and ye shall be pure as thou went out from Me. Let it be known that I am not a fortune of thine imaging, for I am the

ONE which hast given unto the being. I AM thine Father, Source of thine being, so let it be.

I AM and THOU ART, so shall it ever be.

* * * * * * * * * * *

Beloved Ones: This day let it be said that the End Time is shortened, for swiftly approaches the hour when there shall be a great multitude gathered together. And it shall be given unto thee to know the Multitude, and give unto it that which hast been given unto the. I say, as ye have been given, so shall ye give.

Let it be done, for this hast thou been given, that others might be prepared for their part. It is given unto all men to seek the Light, and none shall be denied. So be it that I am the Light. I am sent that ye might have Light - see it and walk ye in it. For this have I called thee out; thou hast heard Me and answered Me. I know wherein thou art staid, and I now say unto thee: Let not thine foot slip, for it is not an easy task to keep thine foot firmly planted upon the path, for there are ones which would direct thee yon way, and they would but beset thee and leave thee without comfort.

I say, they would betray themself without the gold, while there are ones which would sell their birthright for "thirty pieces of silver." Wherein shall they profit? I say, poor in spirit art they. Hear ye Me, and be ye faithful in all things, and I shall reward thee openly. So be it,

I AM Sananda

* * * * * * * * * * *

Be ye as Mine Hand made manifest, and give unto them this Mine Word. Let it be known that I, the Lord thy God, come with the "Rod of Power," and I shall give unto Mine Servants the authority and the power to do Mine Work, for I am not of a mind to go from them in the day of need. I shall give unto them all that which is necessary unto the Work at hand. I say, I know their needs and I am mindful of them, yet I give in Wisdom and Mercy. I know that which is necessary, and it is Mine part to administer unto them. While I give unto them, they give unto the others which have not as yet heard Mine Voice.

I say: As they (the Servants) receive of Me, so do they receive of Mine Servants, and when they have accepted Mine Servants and Mine Word, then I shall quicken them and they, too, shall hear that which I say. For I shall touch them, and they shall be made to hear. Lo, I am come that they be quickened - yet they which set foot against Mine Servants doth set foot against Me, I have spoken out that they might come to know Me, yet I send Mine Servants before Me that they might be prepared to receive Me.

So be it that I see them running after strange gods and seeking signs and wonders. Let them have their strange gods. Yet I say unto all which will: "Come unto Me and I shall give unto thee the keys unto Mine Father's Kingdom." Let them which heareth Mine Voice turn from their wanton and come, and these shall I counsel and these shall I show Mine Hand.

I say unto them: "I am not amongst the Black Magicians, neither am I of the dead! I LIVETH! I LIVETH! I LIVETH! I cry unto thee: "See! Behold the Lord, The Lord of Hosts, The Lord of Lords - Behold This Day - See The Hand of God Move - Rest in Me and be ye made whole, for this have I spoken.

I AM HE which hast been sent of Mine Father that ye be awakened.

So be it, I AM Sananda

* * * * * * * * * * *

Beloved: The hour striketh when there shall be given a Word - THE WORD - which shall fill the air. And The Word shall be as nothing before heard, for man hast not as yet heard the word which shall be spoken. And they shall not know the fullness of it, for they shall be as ones caught unaware. For they have been negligent in their preparation, and at no time have they known the fullness of time. They have speculated, calculated, and measured time by their own measurements; therefore, they shall be found unprepared, for a Mighty Sound shall ring out! It shall fill the air, and it shall shake loose the dead and they shall stand upright and bear witness of the Great Sound - The Word - which no man can translate into his language. For it shall be The Unspeakable Word, that no man be able to translate, for it shall be The Word which hast been held in abeyance for this day.

So great shall be its power that the Mountains shall bow their heads in Holy reverence and the Rivers shall find new bed, for I say unto thee, there shall be a great change, and it shall be for the good of both man and Earth. And man shall awaken and all the Earth shall sing a new song and she, too, shall put on a new garment. For She too shall be baptized into The New Order and she, too, shall rejoice that it is done. For I say unto thee, it shall be a glad day when it is done! So let us rejoice together, for I AM the Lord thy God.

AMEN - AMEN, AND AMEN

* * * * * * * * * * *

Be ye as Mine hand made manifest and record that which I say unto thee, for it is the method which I have chosen by which to reach them which have not the ears to hear. Yet them which do have ears to hear shall hear these Mine Words, and they shall be as ones responsible for that which they do with them. It is said: "Woe unto anyone wheresoever which do spit upon Mine Word." Let it profit them to accept them and to abide thereby.

For it is written that I should come bearing The Rod, "THE ROD OF POWER" - and it is given unto Me to be The Son of The Most High Living God. So be it I come that they might come into the fullness of their estate. While I do not trespass upon their free will, I say unto them: "Come follow ye Me, that I might lead thee out of bondage". So be it, it shall profit thee to follow Me.

Yet there are ones which doth rebel against Mine Sayings. They do resist Me and they persecute Mine Prophets, and they spit upon Mine Word. So be it these I leave. I turn Mine face from them - I give them not of Mine ware. I give unto them nothing which shall be used for the benefit of the dragon, for I simply close Mine door upon them. They are wont to misuse Mine Ware and Mine Word - the gifts which I have. They would misuse the power of the Word - they would use it for their own destruction.

Yet when they will to bring about their own destruction, do not give of Mine time and energy unto their efforts, for I stand ready to give of Mineself when they are of a mind to follow Me.

I call unto them: "COME!" and they resist Me - they deny Me - while they profess to know Me. They call themself Christians? I say they are not with Me; they know Me not. They are the Anti-Christs;

they have not the mind which is in Me. I say, let the mind which is in Me be the mind which is in thee, and then ye shall know wherein thou art staid. So be it I have spoken unto them which have ears which can hear, for none other shall hear for they are the deaf. Let it be for the good of all that I speak, for I Am The Lord Thy God,

Sananda

* * * * * * * * * * *

Hear ye Me and know that I Am the Lord thy God which speaketh unto thee - that which hast gone before thee, that the Way be made clear before thee. I Am He which hast given unto thee the Laws which ye shall apply unto thineself; for thou art not the keeper of thine brother's fortune, thou art not responsible for thine brother's preparation. Inasmuch as he hast free will, he shall do with it as he wills. Yet it is said: "Ye shall be responsible for that which ye do."

It is said: Ye shall make available The Word, and then ye shall not force it upon anyone, for here thine responsibility endeth unto him. While it is thine own responsibility to act in the manner becoming the initiate, the Candidate, it is by example that thine fruit shall be known. It is by example that thou are recognized, not by the words which cometh from out the mouth. While the Candidate walks circumspectly, he, too, sees the power of the Word, and he gives of himself that it be the protection which he asks of Me.

He uses the power allotted unto him for the good of all. Now, let us speak of the protection so desired by them which ask of Me. They speak of the worldly things of man, the "sins" of man, as they would be wont to do of their own, and they reject the Word which I give unto them, for their tongues are cleft. They speak with two tongues: they say that they accept Mine Law, that they are Mine flock, while they revile their fellow men, while they speak words of deceit and hatred, while they pilfer the pockets of their brethren, their fellow beings. They sing hymns of praise unto Me, yet when I say unto them: "Come unto Me and forsake the world of men," they turn not. They stand as ones of stone - they move not.

I say: These are worse than the ones which hast not heard the Law, which hast not proclaimed the Word, which hast not professed The Word or their belief in Me. For to believe upon Me is not to know me; it is NOT to KNOW ME!! For I say, Mine own follow when I call unto them - they know Mine Voice and they follow Me. So be it I say unto the hypocrite: "I speak unto thee - hear ye Me and resist Me not, for the way of the hypocrite, the transgressor, is a sad one. Thine fortune lost, thine lot is cast with the unfortuned ones, thine lot the saddest of them all." So I speak unto the ones which call themself Christ-ians, good; unto them which set themself up and ask of their fellow men alms.

I speak unto them which put a price upon the Word - the Holy Writ - upon the Law which is given thru the prophets sent of God. I say they do miracles in Mine Name; unto all these which do things, lead an unaware people. For they are unaware and know not the difference from the true and the false. Therefore they are gullible. They grab at their bait, and call it good, for it is embellished by their hypocritical word, and they soften it with their own deceit and flowery speech that it might be palatable unto the hungry and thirsty.

I say unto them: "Come, turn from thine folly. Seek not the easy way; first correct thine own errors. Thine own closet shall first be cleansed, then ye shall be acceptable unto Me without a Calling." These

I set Mine foot against, and they shall not set foot upon Mine Altar, for they are impostors and counterfeiters. I say unto them: "These things I abhor, and I give not of Mineself unto them which doth pilfer and adulterate The Word of God, for I come that there be Light - and darkness cometh out of thine adulteration. Give of thineself that ye be cleansed of all thy wanton, then I shall speak with thee."

So be it I AM Sent that here be Light

I AM Sananda, Son of the Most High Living God.

* * * * * * * * * * *

Beloved Children: The whole of Me is that which makes up the whole of the "ALL," yet the All thou dost not see. For the seen part is but the lesser part, the denser part, the heavier outer part, the grosser part which passes away. And it is given unto me to be THAT WHICH PASSES NOT AWAY, for I AM THAT WHICH REMAINS FOREVER, THAT WHICH I AM.

I change not, for I AM THE SOURCE of THAT WHICH IS and that which shall ever BE. And no man can or shall ever create as I, for I AM THE FIRST, THE LAST, THE BEGINNING and THE END, from everlasting unto everlasting. Yea, I AM thine Eternal Self, thine Eternal BEing, I Am all that thou shall ever BE. I AM the FATHER, MOTHER, the SON, and outside ME no thing exists which IS. For that matter, that which is of <u>non</u>-existence is but the illusion created by man in his blindness, in his blundering and wandering in bondage, darkness.

I say: It is his own illusion which hast blinded him, and it shall pass as <u>no</u>-thing - be as nothing, for it has not existed in the realm of Reality. It is of the world of illusion which has no reality. I say unto thee, Mine

Children: I have given unto thee all that which I AM, for it is Mine Nature that I create perfect and whole. Yet thou hast divided thineself into "parts" - classes, families, nations, principalities, ideologies, and into faiths concerning thine Creator - thine being, thine doing, thine coming. Thine own belief hast been unto thee great torment, for thou hast believed many things which have been thine own downfall, thine own undoing. For thou hast given power unto the Dragon - I say, thou hast given unto him power over thee, and he is of man's own creation. This thing which man hast created is now prepared to swallow him up!

Yet I say unto Mine Children: He, this thine own creation, this thine own creature which thou hast fashioned out of thine own offal, shall be seen for that which he is. Now, ye shall turn thine face homeward and give unto him no power over thee, for he hast no power over thee.

I speak unto thee as thine Father Eternal. Arise ye and come home. Let them which have ears to hear, hear Mine Word and Come, for I shall not turn them away.

Solen Aum Solen

* * * * * * * * * * *

Beloved Ones: There is much unrest within the world of men, and they know not where to turn. They look hither and yon, yet they find no peace, for peace is not within them. They go about as robots; they ask of men peace - yet I say, man is incapable of giving unto them peace, for they first have to establish peace within themself. For peace is not to be found in the world of men, for it is the way of man that he hast accepted that he make wars, that he put his foot against his brother.

While I say unto them, peace shall first be established within thine own heart - and then ye shall know peace - for Mine Peace ye shall know,

Now let it be said that peace comes from knowing thine Self to be one with God The Father, and poise follows such knowing. It lies not within the power of man to establish peace within the heart of another, for the peace of which I speak is a gift, and thou alone can put thine finger upon it. I say, take it, prepare thine own house.

Then ask of others that they might find thine own house in order." Come, partake of Mine Household", then they shall see that thou hast thine own house in order - and therein they shall partake of thine own gifts which shall be unto them an example. I say, first set thine own house in order, O man of Earth, then ye shall partake of our knowledge, of our hospitality. Then we shall accept thee into the Assembly of the Brothers, which have held out a hand unto thee lo these many centuries. I say: Blest are they which have accepted it, for he shall find Peace. So be it that I am come that the Way be made strait before thee.

So be it. I AM Sananda

* * * * * * * * * * *

Sornica

Sori Sori: All Hail! Hail unto The King! The King of Kings - HE IS COME! See the Power made manifest in the world of the seen. For it shall be made manifest upon the Earth even as it is in Heaven.

For I say unto thee: "He hast Come to claim His own; He hast come to gather up His Own, and He shall not be denied.

Hail! Hail! He hast Come. Be ye as one prepared to receive Him, for He shall reveal Himself unto them which are so prepared to receive Him.

Be ye amongst them which hast put on the Royal Raiment. Come ye forth as the ones prepared to enter into the Holy of Holies with Him, for He hast called thee forth. Stand guard and let thine Light so shine that all might see it and be drawn unto it. I say unto thee, let it be known, HE IS COME, THE KING OF KINGS.

Sornica

* * * * * * * * * * *

Beloved of Mine Being: This day I would speak of the power of The Word - and the Word is but the Power sent forth from out the mouth of THE MOST HIGH LIVING GOD. It is the power thru, and by which all things are set into motion. For motion follows the Word and The Word of God precedes the motion which brings forth that which is made manifest in the world of manifestation. Sing ye praise unto Him, for He hast given unto thee the mountain top, the valley at its foot.

He hast given unto thee the mighty Aspen, the foot of which is planted upon the Earth; and it hast its counterpart within the realms above, which are far more beautiful than within thine own realm, which is but the denser part, the counterpart of the Real. I say unto thee, thine eyes shall be opened up unto the REAL of thine world, and ye shall see that which thou hast not seen, for the ETH shall reveal unto thee that which it holds for thee, for it is the unseen which shall be made seen - the unknown which shall be made known. And at no time shall these things be revealed unto the unjust, for they are the things within Mine keeping, and I am not to be found wanting.

I shall open wide the door, and I bid thee enter in, all ye which are so prepared - so be it I know thine preparation, thine strength. I Come that ye be strengthened and that ye might partake of Mine fortune. Now I say unto thee: Count thineself fortunate that I have touched upon this subject, for it is written: "All which are so prepared may enter into Mine place of Abode."

So be it. I AM the Lord thy God, Sananda

* * * * * * * * * * *

Beloved Ones: This is Mine day and I say unto thee: Mine time is come when I shall go forth openly, and I shall declare unto all men that I AM COME. I shall give unto them as they are prepared to receive, and there are ones which have asked of Me - these shall not be denied.

I say unto thee: I shall not be hidden in a corner, neither shall I be put into a closet! I am come that all men might be lifted up. So be it that I shall go into every land, unto every people, and I shall find them which ask of Me. These I shall give unto and these shall I give in great measure. I shall perform a mighty work, and man shall come into his own, for long hast he been as one bound - bound down by his own legirons. Now, it is come when he shall arise and cast them off, and he shall walk upright as a free man and at no time shall I turn Mine back upon him which hast a mind to follow where I lead him.

So be it. I AM Sananda

* * * * * * * * * * *

Sori Sori: Let this be a day of rejoicing, for I, the Lord thy God, speaks unto thee out of the fullness of Mine Love, and for that have I said unto thee: "I shall not forsake thee". I shall give unto thee that which is necessary unto thine progress. I shall not burden thee with great and lengthy sermons. I shall give unto thee that which thou needst for thine fulfillment, the fulfillment of thine Mission, I tell thee that Mind hand is not shortened. Mine time is come, and at no time shall I be caught off guard!

It is said, I am sufficient unto the day. Be ye alert unto that which I give unto thee and fret not over the things which they do, for it is not given unto thee to be thine brother's keeper. Thine brother hast a will of his own - betray it not, for I say unto thee, he alone is responsible for that which he does. Be ye responsible for that which ye do.

For that do I say unto thee: Be ye as a Beacon set upon a hill that they might see thine Light and be drawn unto it. Walk ye with surety and heed that which I say unto thee. Walk with thine brother, yet let him choose that way which he goes - be ye not the one to choose his way. When he departs from thee, speak of him as he hast witnessed the Word, the Work which I have done, and judge him not. By his own mouth and actions shall he judge himself - he alone shall be the judge. Ask naught of him, for he hast not as yet learned full well his responsibility. Be ye as ones prepared to accept the responsibility which shall be given unto thee. Ye shall carry it with dignity and with Great Stature - for this have I sibored thee.

I AM Sananda

* * * * * * * * * * *

Beloved Ones: Present thineself as a living sacrifice before the Most High Living God, and be ye as ones prepared to receive of Him that which is thine Divine inheritance. (say unto thee, there is nothing which shall be withheld from thee. All things shall be made known unto thee and ye shall be as ones prepared to sibor them which are yet to be risen, for they, too, shall follow thee even as thou hast followed Me.

I say, it is like unto a chain - a chain command: as each link moves forward, another moves up into its proper place or position. Even so with the Earth: as one planet moves out, She, the Earth, shall move forward to become a shining orb unto lesser planets - some yet unformed. I say unto thee, great things are in store for thee - yet this is the day of preparation, and it is the day of testing and proving. The Earth is "The Proving Ground," and it hast served thee well, for many lessons it hast held for thee - many lessons yet unrevealed. Yet, thou hast not fathomed its Mysteries.

I say, ye shall come to know the depth of her Mysteries well. I say, ye shall rejoice in the store of wealth which she shall open up unto thee. So be it that I shall touch the Door and it shall swing wide before thine eyes; and ye shall behold the glory of "Her Store," for long hast she held the Mysteries of the ages. Behold ye the "Mysteries revealed" - for I say unto thee, these shall be revealed. Let it serve thee well - I am come that it be so.

I AM Sananda

* * * * * * * * * * *

Sori Sori: Hold ye high the Banner which I bring - hold ye fast! Let not the way of man deceive thee; be ye alert unto their way and let not them deceive thee. For it is said, they have the fortune of the dragon; they are wont to show themself as wise and strut and parade themself before man that they might be praised of men, that they might be called great, that they might be honored of men.

I say: Look! See! and behold them in their foolishness. They know not that they shall be caught up short. I say, they shall be brot to account for their foolishness.

This is the Day of Accounting, the Day of Work, and the Day of Contemplation, for it behooves them to give of themself that they might be prepared for the days ahead, the time at hand. It is fortuned unto Me to know that which lies just ahead. Yet they go headlong, giving unto Me no thot! I cry aloud: "Be ye about thine preparation, thine salvation! Come ye out from among them and be ye separate. Be ye as one which hast the mind to take up Mine Banner and follow Me that ye might go where I go." So be it that I Am the Lord thy God and I know where I go, and I, too, know where the pitfalls lie.

So be it I ask of thee naught save obedience unto the Law. Harken ye, and be ye as one alert - each unto his own preparation; each shall be his own carter, none shall bring him against his will. Yet I say, lay aside thine foolish ways, thine self, and come as an empty vessel. And I shall give unto thee that which shall satisfy thee and that which shall be unto thee free passport into the place wherein I abide.

Let it be as the Father hast willed it.

I AM Sananda

* * * * * * * * * * *

Beloved Ones: While it is given unto thee to be of the Great and Mighty Host, I say unto thee, I Am the Lord of Hosts, and for this do I say unto thee that I Am qualified for Mine part. And I am aware of that which goes on in the world of men, in the realms of Spirit, and at no time is anything hidden from Me. It is for this that I am prepared to reveal unto thee that which shall be revealed unto thee.

For the good of all shall it be; yet I say unto thee, be ye as ones prepared with Wisdom, and with the Wisdom of Mine shall ye give unto others that which I shall reveal unto thee. For there are ones which would misuse the part which would be unto thee great Power and Light, great Knowledge. Yet they would rend thee with such power, for they have not yet learned the First Lesson - that of Love. So be ye as wise as the Serpent; give unto them with Wisdom.

Bear in mind there are ones which are sent forth to build up, others to tear down, and ye shall know them for that which they are. So be it that I Know Them, and it is now come when they shall be brot to account, for their nefarious plans shall fail. I have spoken and thou hast heard Me.

I AM Sananda

* * * * * * * * * * *

Beloved Ones: While I say unto thee this is the day of Thanksgiving, let it be, for it is so - It Is So! And it is fortuned unto thee to be as ones which have many Blessings bestowed upon thee - yet thou knowest not that which is in store for thee. I say, even greater than thou hast imaged. I say unto thee, behold the Word of God made manifest; see it made manifest before thee. Sing ye songs of praise - let thine heart sing and be ye glad. Rest in the knowing that I Am Come. I Am with thee and rejoice that it is so. Be ye about the business at hand, and let thine feet be swift to do that which I give unto thee to do. Praise ye the Name of Solen Aum Solen, and be ye as ones filled with Love, for Love abideth forever. Hear ye Mine Words and rejoice that ye have heard. And I shall speak again and again.

I AM Sananda

* * * * * * * * * * * *

Beloved Ones: There are many which await this Mine Word. I say unto thee, ye shall give it unto them which ask - the ones which are of a mind to receive of Me and it shall profit them.

Say unto them in Mine Name that I am Come - I AM COME! I come that they might go where I go. So be it I am not of the Earth - I am free, free from all bonds. I give not unto the forces of darkness that it/they be strengthened - yet I deny not that which serves to lift man up. I give of Mineself that they be lifted - have they understood that which I say? Nay, they have not! They have not heard Mine Words, for they have not given unto Me credit for being that which I AM.

They seek safety? security? Wherein have they found it? Wherein have they been prepared for this Day? It is now come upon them when they shall seek a place of safety - yet they know not which way. It is given unto Me to see them faint and fall by the way. Yet it is said, the path of Initiation is strewn with the bones of the ones which wearied of their climb. I send not one to carry them in. They come by their own effort; they prepare themself, then they are given assistance. For they alone are responsible for their preparation. After that, We of the Higher

Order give unto them which are of a mind to receive. So be it that I am come that they might receive the Greater part/their inheritance in full.

So be it they now go forth seeking freedom of men/asking of men while they are filled with hatred and anger. They are affright; they are in no wise prepared to receive Me. They give unto Me the dregs of their own cup. They forget the hunger of the poor; they administer not unto their needs, as brothers. They gorge their bellies; they satisfy their appetites; they sing their songs to Me.

For their own ears they sing; unto themself they give praise. They speak of Me, yet they follow not Mine precepts, neither do they follow Me. I say, their hypocrisy is an abomination in Mine sight. I say, Love ye one another, yet they war - they slay the lesser brother that their appetites be satisfied. They are guilty of Murder! And I see them as murderers, tormentors! I see them as hypocrites! I am not deceived by their appearance, their tinsel and baubles/their paint and powder/their furbish.

I say, come unto me as a living sacrifice, as a clean vessel, that I might come in and sup with thee. I go not into the dragon's den; I bear witness of Mine Father - I bring Light. I Am The Light and The Way. Deceive not thineself, O ye hypocrites, ye murderers, ye purveyors of lies!

I know wherein thou abideth. I know thee, and I shall mark thee, and I shall show thee unto Mine People, for that which thou art. I shall protect Mine People from thee. I say, thine days are near unto the end, for ye shall not bind Mine People longer by thine nefarious schemes. I say unto thee, O black dragon: BEGONE! BE YE GONE!! LET MINE PEOPLE GO!

I have spoken and I have been heard - so shall it be, for I have spoken with Power and Truth. Let it be heard in all the Earth!

I AM Sananda

* * * * * * * * * * *

This day let it be recorded for all which are of a mind to see, to know that which I say unto thee. For it is for the good of all mankind that I speak out; and for the Great Brotherhood of man that they be lifted up, that they be brot out of bondage and that they might come unto the fullness of their Inheritance. Let it be known that there is a place provided for them - a place wherein they might go as Sons of God wherein they might be at peace.

I say unto thee this day that there is no peace within the world of men, wherein they are prepared to destroy all mankind by their foolishness. I say, by their foolishness are they prepared to destroy themself. Yet I say unto thee, there are none prepared to give unto thee life, for they are not the givers of life.

Let it be said, they cannot destroy life. They can but destroy the outward forms of manifestation - that which hast form/that which is manifest in flesh/that which hast form in the world of manifestation the seen world/the world which is within the third dimension which is the world which is known unto men of flesh. Yet I say unto thee, this is only the lesser/the lower/the outer, and not the Eternal.

For the forms shall pass and be no more, while the Eternal shall ever BE and be no less for having taken form - forms of flesh, or that of the seen world. Spirit is Spirit and no less for having taken upon itself forms. While I say Spirit animates the form and is no less for having form within the dense world of form, let it be understood that thou art Eternal Beings, born of God The Eternal Father, and thou art Light Substance - born of Light. From the beginning hast thou been made in the Likeness of His Image, and He hast Imaged thee perfect from the beginning. So be it ye shall return unto Him even as thou went out. So be it. I have spoken and thou hast heard Me.

I AM the Lord thy God

* * * * * * * * * * * *

Beloved Ones: I Am the One Sent that this word might be given unto thee, and it shall be for the good of all mankind. It shall profit them which ask of thee that they might read these Mine words.

I say: All which ask shall be given, and unto them which misuse them I say: "Pity art thou," for the poor in spirit shall hunger for the bread of life, and it shall be given unto him, yet he shall not spit upon it.

While it is Mine part to say unto thee: "Thou art now the Sons of God," it hast always been so. Yet it behooves Me to say: "Thou art Sons of the Light, SONS OF THE MOST HIGH LIVING GOD." So be it I Am come this day that ye might know thine true identity - thine true self - the imperishable Self. For this I am come, and I say unto thee, I shall touch thee and ye shall know. So be it that I shall give of Mineself that ye might know. So be it. I Am the Lord thy God.

Sananda

* * * * * * * * * * * *

Sori Sori: Hail! Hail! unto the Victor! Hail all ye Sons of God - Hail, Hail unto the King! The King of Glory! Hail unto the Host - the Mighty Council, the Mighty Ones which stand by, that ye be assisted in thine ascent. Be ye blest as They are blest for I say unto thee, they are blest. They are blest indeed! for theirs is a great Service - Theirs is a service little known by man of Earth.

For They are not the Ones to parade Themself before man that he be impressed of Their powers, their wisdom. They move supremely, with wisdomed grace, at all times on the beam - They blunder not! They know what they go out to do, and they are a patient lot. They are not, for that matter, of the earthlings. They are of another part of the Great Mansion which man knows so little of. For that matter I might say nothing, for his knowledge comes thru and by revelation which is limited. For he which thinks himself wise is the most limited by his own opinions and preconceived ideas.

I Am Come that man might come into the fullness of his heritage, yet he has the desire to go his way in darkness - his own way is darkness, for his is the way of flesh. While he knows nothing of "The Law" (the law by which We have Our Being), he asks not of his Source for his learning. He asks of man and his opinion/his theories, while he speaks of and about the things of great import. He knows not the meaning of the "Greater Part" - that which is Light, Love, Peace - and at no time has he established within himself peace, for peace is not within him. While he says "Peace," peace is no part of him.

I say unto thee: "Peace," for peace is Mine. I know peace - I AM PEACE, and peace is Mine to give. Yet I say, "Come unto me and I shall give unto thee peace," and unto all that hear Mine Voice and harken unto it, I shall give unto him as I have received of Mine Father.

So be it I say: "Come all ye that are weary, and I shall give unto thee of Mine peace."

So be it. I AM Sananda

* * * * * * * * * * * *

Hold ye high the Banner which I bring; lay aside thine preconceived ideas of the Lord, for the Way of the Lord is the way of Spirit. Spirit is the way in which ye shall go, for flesh is but a fleeting thing, while Spirit is everlasting. I say: Be ye as the one prepared to see and know what goes on in the realm of Spirit. I say, Spirit takes unto itself that which is of dense substance called "matter," and it is for this that I say unto thee: "Fear not that which shall come upon thee, for Spirit is ever Spirit and can be no less for having taken up a garment of flesh as dense substance." While it is but a fleeting thing, I tell thee for a surety it is the lesser.

The lesser shall have no reality when thou hast passed from it (the body of dense matter). I say unto thee, Fear Not, for it is but the beginning of thine new part. So be it I say unto all which are fortuned these Words: Fear Not, for change is good. Let it be so with thee, for I have come that it might be well with thee; so let it be.

I AM Sananda

* * * * * * * * * * * *

Be ye as one blest this day, for I am come that ye be blest. Let it be, for it is now come when ye shall bring many out of darkness; I say, ye shall bring many out of darkness. Ye shall be a lamp unto their feet - yet ye shall not trespass upon their free will. Ye shall be unto them a lamp, and they shall see the Light thereof. Ye shall stand as Sentinel upon the hilltop, and ye shall give no quarter, neither shall ye take any quarter. Ye shall stand firm and be as The Rock, for so firmly shall thine feet be planted upon the Rock Which I AM, neither wind, rain, nor fire shall come nigh unto thee - ye shall endure! For this have I sibored thee in the Way of the Lord.

Give unto them which ask, that which I give unto thee for them. Yet ye shall allow them their own way/will, and ye shall condemn them not, for all are not of a mind to come unto Me. These shall wait; they shall wait; while their waiting shall be long and hard, they alone shall learn the lesson of waiting. It is said: "This is the day of preparation," and it is so. This day they prepare the environment for the new place of abode, for each shall be placed in his own environment which he hast created for himself. Each unto his own - so be it the Law. I come that there be Light - that the Law be fulfilled - that I might gather up Mine Own. I shall find them which are prepared to receive Me, for I know them by their Light.

Let thine own Light so shine that I might find thee and I shall touch thee, and ye shall be quickened, and ye shall know me as I know thee. So be it and Selah.

I AM Sananda

* * * * * * * * * * *

Beloved Ones: This day I say unto thee: "Peace, Peace, Peace - Mine Peace I give unto thee. Give of thineself that there be Peace - let it be." While they cry for Peace, I say: "Be ye at Peace" - yet they hear Me not! While they cry out for light, I say: "Come unto Me, for I AM THE

LIGHT - I AM THE LIGHT" - yet they hear Me not. I say, hear ye Me and come unto Me, O ye children of Earth, for I stand ready to lift thee up. So be it I Am one of the Mighty Host. I Am The One Sent that ye be brot out of bondage; yet ye seek after strange gods and seek signs and wonders. O ye children of Earth, hear ye Me and be ye as ones which have a mind to comprehend that which I say unto thee. Be ye blest to hear, for I Am The Lord thy God.

Sananda

* * * * * * * * * * *

Beloved Ones: Many there be which have given of their talents, love, and time that this day come into the fullness, that this day might bring forth new fruit. Now, I say unto thee, ye shall bear witness of Mine Word, and ye shall know that I have said unto thee these things. I say unto thee this day that there are great things in store for thee, and greater than thou hast dreamed of. While it is yet the early morning of this new day, I say that the Sun rises upon a new day, and at its height it shall be as nothing before seen upon the Earth. For there shall be great hiways and byways which shall be deserted - obsolete; while there shall be greater and more glorious hiways, wherein mankind shall move in the flash of sound.

At the speed of sound shall he move, and in these hiways there shall be no odor, no motors, clumsy and heavy, to the detriment of their swiftness. These shall be as man hast not as yet imaged. While I say unto thee, one shall come into the Earth with such knowledge, and he shall bring forth the work which shall bring this about. While man hast struggled long in his own stupid way, he shall now ask for greater knowledge; and one shall come, and he shall bring with him this knowledge. Let it suffice that he is now ready and prepared to make his appearance, and it shall be for the good of all mankind. So be it that I have touched upon a new subject. Yet I shall say more; wait upon Me and I shall speak unto thee again. I Am the One known as The Architect of The New Dispensation. Fortune thineself this knowledge which I have given unto thee.

* * * * * * * * * * *

Beloved Ones: I speak unto thee this day of the work which is yet to be done; and it shall be given unto thee to have part in the plan which unfolds before thee. It is for this that I say unto thee: Stand ye steadfast - let thine hand be Mine, thine mind be Mine, thine feet be Mine, and ye shall not fail. Behold in Me the Light which I AM, and ye shall walk with surely and stumble not.

For this have I prepared a part for thee, this part which I now proffer unto thee. Accept it in Mine Name, and be ye as one blest. Ask of no man his opinion, his blessing. I say unto thee, bless thineself that others be blest, for I so prepare thee that ye might bless them. Hold high Mine Lamp - the Lamp which I give unto thee casts no shadows before it, and they shall see the Light.

They shall be as ones come from afar to pay homage unto thee, for they are now as the waters tossed upon the winds. They are a restless lot, knowing not whither to turn. Yet they shall find the Light which shall not be denied them. They shall come crying for surcease from their woes. Let it be given unto them to receive it in Mine Name, and at no time shall I deny then which seeketh the Light. Let it be given as they can comprehend for this have I spoken unto thee. They shall find solace, and PEACE shall be established within them.

Be ye as ones alert and fortune unto thineself the greater part. Pass not unto another thine own cup until it is purified and made perfect. Force not upon another thine opinions, thine preconceived ideas. Let thine own cup be clean, and it shall be fit for thine brother; then he, too, shall be filled and satisfied. Let no man give unto thee the dregs of his own cup which he hast given unto himself/fortuned unto himself. For 1 say unto thee, first seek the Light and all things shall be given unto thee which is necessary for thine Salvation. I say, Behold The Light which I AM, for I Am the Lord thy God. See the Light and walk ye in it, and I shall come in and abide with thee.

So be it. I AM Sananda

* * * * * * * * * * *

Be ye as Mine hand made manifest and give unto them this Word, and say as I would that there are Mighty Ones which stand by to assist in the "Last Days" which is now come. And it shall bring with it the Signs of the times; and it shall be as the Handwriting on the wall. I say unto thee: Look! See that which is written thereupon, for it shall be revealed unto thee. Look! See and read, for it shall be given unto thee to read and ye shall know the meaning thereof. So be it and Selah.

I am He which is sent that ye might know.

I AM Sananda

* * * * * * * * * * *

Be ye as ones prepared for the things which have been foretold are upon thee, and at no time shall We be found to give unto thee erroneous counsel. For I say: We forewarn thee that which ye shall do and the results thereof.

It is said: "Prepare thineself and ye shall not want." Ye Shall be as ones which have given heed unto that which hast been said, and ye shall be given assistance - and at no time shall ye be given the bitter cup. Yet ye shall be as ones prepared to accept us and receive of us. For I say unto thee: We know thine preparation wherein thou art prepared; We hear thine call and know that which ye ask. We know that which prompts thine call. Yet it shall be fortuned unto us, thine Benefactors, to give unto thee in wisdom and justice as thou art prepared to receive - so be it just. Let it be said that suffering makes of all men brothers.

I AM Sananda

* * * * * * * * * * * *

Beloved Ones: Mind hand is firm and strong, and I forget not that which I have said unto thee - I forget not!

Let thine hand be swift to feed Mine flock, for this have I given unto thee these portions. Yet I say unto them which would spit upon them or misuse them, they shall be brot to account for their foolishness. For these Portions are the Word of Life, living Words, Words by which they shall be brot out of bondage.

Harden not thine heart. Turn not a deaf ear unto Mine Words, for I have spoken and I am speaking, and I shall speak again and again, until every ear doth hear, and even unto the dead shall they awaken and come forth! For I shall send forth a Mighty One which shall sound the last trumpet, and in that day even the dead shall come forth. So be it I have spoken and thou hast heard Me; let them which have ears hear and be blest. So be it and Selah.

I AM Sananda

* * * * * * * * * * *

Behold ye this day the Wonders of the Lord thy God. Behold ye the dawn: see the Light which I AM. Bathe ye in the waters of life which I AM. Sing ye a joyful song, and let it be that which I have sung. Let it be Mine Song, for it is the eternal praise unto the Father which hast brot us hence. Be ye mindful of His love and mercy, for I say unto thee, it exceeds all that which man hast imaged; for man knows not such love and mercy. Be ye as ones blest, and remember thine blessings.

Count them one by one - then ye shall count them ten by ten. Fortune unto thineself such knowledge as I, for to know is to be as "The One." To know is to be wise, and it is the wise which know. Forgive the foolish their unknowing - forgive them their foolishness. They, too, shall come to know in time, for I say, they are bound by time. And it is said: Time shall be no more - So let it pass. Hear ye Me and be ye blest this day.

I AM Sananda

* * * * * * * * * * *

Beloved Ones: While it is given unto thee to be silent, there are ones which are not silent. There are ones which shout their words from the house tops, and these are as the foolish virgins which have no oil. They have not tasted of Mine Cup; they know not the joy which is Mine; they have not as yet heard Mine Voice. They but speak that which they have pilfered - that which is written - that which others have said unto them. Theirs is a puny part, for it is not of Me. They have not as yet touched the hem of Mine Garment.

So be it I say unto them: "Seek ye the Light and fortune unto thineself the greater part. Then I shall touch thee - and I knoweth thine capacity." Let thine own Cup be filled, and then they shall become aware of the overflow. Let thine Light so shine that they might see it and know that thou hast had communion with Me. So be it. I Am the Lord thy God.

I AM Sananda

* * * * * * * * * * *

Be ye as Mine Mouth/Mine Voice and say unto them as i would that the time is come when a great force shall be unleashed upon them and they shall find no hiding place. Then they shall cry for help; yet I say unto them, they have been warned and warned again. Now, it shall come upon them as a thief in the night, and they shall find themself trapt as rats. Yet they have not heeded Mine Words: "Prepare thineself." They have played the Piper's tune; they have danced to the fiddlers while they have chosen their own music - the song of Satan. They have paid the price of the fiddlers; they have sold their inheritance for a poor penny and they shall be brot to account for their folly.

I say, Poor foolish mortals! Poor foolish mortals they be; they stand as with feet of lead. They are as ones bound by their legirons: they move not; they are trapt!

I say: I am come that they might be loosed; yet they fear the Light. They ask of man's opinions, and man is subject to such foolishness and asks of another, while I say: "Seek ye the Light, and it shall not be denied thee; trust not in the arm of flesh, for flesh is weak."

I say unto thee: "Ask of no man his opinion." Let it be for thine own sake that I say unto thee: "Seek ye the Light," and I shall send unto thee a Host which shall assist. So be ye blest as I am blest.

I AM the Lord thy God, Sananda

* * * * * * * * * * *

Be ye as ones prepared that ye might bear witness of Me, for I shall make Mineself manifest into the world of the seen, and it shall be as none hast imaged, for I shall do a Work unknown unto any man. I shall put forth Mine hand, and they which are so prepared might touch it, and they shall know for a surety they have touched Me. It shall be given unto them to know, for they shall be quickened and they shall not doubt, for I shall give unto them comprehension.

I say, they shall know the true from the false. So be it that I am the One Sent that they might know. Let it be a time of fulfillment - for this I have waited. Let every man which hast eyes to see, SEE; every man which hast ears to hear, HEAR. For this have I spoken the Word "PREPARE." For this have I said: "Prepare thineself" - so be it. I am not mocked. I, too, say that I shall walk amongst them, and some there be which know Me not, while there shall be some which are prepared to receive Me - so be it. These shall touch, and they shall be quickened; so let it be well with thee.

I AM Sananda

* * * * * * * * * * *

Blest art they which come unto this Altar. Blest art they which receive of the Lord God, Sent of Mine Father. Blest are they which give of themself that others receive of Me. Blest are they which have been given the privilege of coming into this place, for I say unto thee: This is Mine House - I have founded it - I have builded it upon The Rock. I have set it apart from the world.

I have set it as a beacon on a hill; I have provided it, and I have fortuned unto it that which is wise and necessary unto its fulfillment. I have given generously that it be kept in order, that it be supplied. have been unto it the Source of supply. I have been generous with Mine hand, with Mine Word, and I have forced upon thee great learning and great wisdom. While thou hast not known the fullness of Mine Word, I say unto thee, it shall profit thee to heed every Word, for it is given for a purpose. And I know the wisdom thereof/the purpose; and for that have I given it in like manner. So let it go forth that they which receiveth might profit thereby. Let it be heard thruout the land: He is come! He Is Come - the King of Kings - The Lord of Lords. For it is said: He which IS COME is the Lord of Lords - the King of Kings!

It is I, The Lord thy God, Sananda

* * * * * * * * * * *

Be ye as the one set apart from this Mine part which I shall dictate unto thee; and for this hast thou been prepared. I say unto thee: This part which I shall dictate unto thee shall be as nothing thou hast had, for it is a part separate and different from all other parts.

I say unto thee: Each part is carefully prepared, carefully given, and carefully it is received. Yet it is given unto man to be as one critical of the method - the way in which it is written, for he sees not beyond the letter. I say, the letter is but means of the blind seeing that which hast been given unto them, thru one which sees with the "Single Eye." And they which have the Single Eye see that which is said thru the Spirit, for they are but forms which are meant to convey the true meaning of The Word.

The idea expressed is not the letter, yet they seek out "The Letter," thus tripping over Mine meaning. Thus hast it ever been with the ones which think themself wise. While they flounder and drown in shallow waters, I shall take thee out into deeper waters wherein ye shall walk with surety. So be it that I shall lead thee, and ye shall not fall. So be it that I have given unto thee a word (omitted), and ye shall remember it, for it is given for a purpose, and it shall be added to.

Yet it shall not be given out unto them which know not its meaning, for the misuse of such is not well; for to use such as this is fortuned unto them which set themself up. They think to pilfer the "Magic" of these sacred words which doth rebound upon them, bringing great woe; for the Sacred Word carries great power, and the misuse thereof brings much sorrow. While in their unknowing and in their zeal to do these things, they are as the child which knows not.

While the child which uses the match for his own learning finds that it burns, for he hast not learned the "magic" thereof - the power - the proper use of it. Let this be as a word to the wise; pilfer not the sayings of the wise. Pilfer not the Sacred Symbols given unto the Sibets - the ones which are of a mind to follow Me - for I say: "Thou which hast set thine hand unto the plow and dost turn back shall fall." I say: Look ye where I lead thee, walk ye as ones sober, and be diligent in thine work, for I say: Many say Lord! Lord! and they wait not upon

Me. I hear them and I wait. I wait for them that they might prove themself trustworthy - that they be prepared to receive Me and of Me.

So be it I have spoken unto Mine Servants; I have spoken unto them which cry Lord! Lord! and wait not for Me to answer. I say: I know them, and I am not slow in Mine Father's business - I am alert! I know them; I know the meaning of their words, that which prompts them. Their sayings availeth them nothing, for 1 am not so foolish as to be moved by their vain repetitions. I wait for them to prepare the House of the Lord that I might enter in. I say, their vain repetitions shall not be given credence, for I know that which prompts them. I am not a foolish "Parson," neither do I indulge them with soothing platitudes and sweet words of comfort. I come not to comfort; I come that they be brot out of bondage. So be it.

I AM the Lord thy God, Sananda

* * * * * * * * * * *

Dare they trespass upon the House of God? Dare they resist the Word of God? For long hast it been said, they shall not pass the port of their own limits without the proper credentials. I say, it is given unto Me to know, for I am One alert and I know that which goes on - I am not to be caught off guard. It is given unto man to forget that which hast been said, and it is his way that he war against his brother, Yet he goes far afield in quest of new horizons which he thinks to lay claim upon.

Hear ye, O man of Earth, it is said that thou all not escape the Law, for it is the Law which binds the heavens and the Earth. For that matter, Love is the cohesive power of the planetary systems - systems untold - and love thou hast not known! For love is the ever existing power which holds the planets within their courses. I say unto thee: "Think ye to rebel against such a force?" I say unto thee: Thine time is come! Ye shall be caught up short, for no man rebelleth without the consequence.

I tell thee of a surety: Love is the cohesive power which holds the planets within their course, and thou hast not learned the first principle of Love. While it is said: "The way of the transgressor is hard," it is so, and none shall escape the Law. Let it be understood that man is but the ones which have the mind and the free will granted him by the Mercy and Grace of Our Father Which hast given unto them being.

So be it that they are wont to give unto themself credit for being wise. Yet they are not so wise when they take unto themself all the credit; yet they take not the credit for all the suffering which is brot about by their transgressions. Woe unto them which transgress the law.

I say unto them: "Prepare thineself that ye might be acceptable unto the Great and Mighty Council, and then ye shall pass into the next door." Yet ye shall find that ye have not prepared thineself, and ye shall find the door closed unto thee as an undesirable lot. I speak fearlessly and plainly, for I am not a fearsome man. I speak of Spirit and as Spirit! I am not amongst the dead! I am the Head of The Mighty Council, and I know the Law, for I am at this for long ages untold.

I am the Lord of Hosts, the Lord of Lords, and I compromise not with the lesser, for I am come that I might bring Light into the darkness. While the darkness comprehends not the Light, I say: Mine Own shall see it and follow it, and after I have taken out Mine Own, I shall then do unto the others that which I must. And they shall be of the same nature still, for it is given unto them to rebel against the Law. Therefore, they know Me not, and they have not the mind to follow Me. Yet Mine hand shall move thru all the lands, and it shall not be staid! Awaken! Awaken all ye men of Earth! and stand forth as ones alert! For I say unto thee: The Voice shall be raised and ye shall know that I, the Lord thy God, hast spoken. So let thine ears be attuned, for this have I spoken.

I AM Sananda

* * * * * * * * * * *

Beloved: It is the time that is long foretold when great sorrow shall come upon the people and when they shall cry Lord! Lord! This is the time of stress and it is the time when great turmoil shall be their lot. For I say unto thee: These people which now inhabit the lands of the Earth are the ones which hast fashioned this day. It is their lot, for they have caused it to be; it is the day which they have fashioned. This is their accumulated fortune. The word hast been spoken and it hast gone out and returned unto them as a great black dragon which would consume them.

Now, I say unto them: Come! Come! turn from thine own creation which wouldst devour thee. And ye shall give unto the Father credit for thine being and give unto Him thine will, and He shall give unto thee as thou art prepared to receive. I say: He shall not deny thee thine inheritance, yet ye shall be as one prepared to receive it.

This is the day of sifting, sorting, weighing, accounting and reckoning. Let it profit thee, for I say unto thee: Ponder well Mine sayings - deny them not - think not thou art finished, for I say unto thee, it is not so. Be ye alert, and fashion not thine own legirons - cut them away and be ye free, even as I am free. I go and come freely. I am not bound by creed, dogma or any of man's opinions. I am one with Mine Father and I do His will without hesitation, without effort or thot, for I am one with Him.

I give unto Him credit for that which I AM. I wait not for man, yet I am come that man might become as I AM. Yet I pass, I come, and when the time is come that the door is closed, I shall leave as I have come (for the Earth is not Mine abiding place).

And then they shall cry unto Me unheard! for I shall go unto Mine Father which hast sent Me, and no more shall I come unto the Earth that they be brot out of bondage.

Nay, sayeth man - the one which thinks he is wise. I say: Man knoweth not the plan, for I reveal not the plan unto the wanton; the uninitiated knoweth not any portion of the great plan which I have within Mine hand. I am the Director of this New Dispensation and I know that which I am about, for I am prepared for Mine part for long, and I stand ready to assist in any way, any place, any time in this Divine Plan.

Now, I say: The time swiftly comes when the ones which have not accepted Mine hand shall be cut off. They shall be given a place and a time: the place shall be unto them that which they have prepared for themself; the time shall be as it is according unto the Law.

And they shall know much stress - much sorrow - and they shall be faced with their Shame, for Shame it is. I say: They have denied their inheritance, and they have dined sumptuously on the husks from the belly of the swine.

It is a day of choosing, a day of finish, a day of opening up for the ones which hast heard and heeded Mine Word. Let it be heard - for this is it spoken.

I AM Sananda

* * * * * * * * * * *

Beloved of Mine Being: Let it be said that there are many which come into the Earth at this time for the purpose of assisting in the Great Plan, which is designed to assist all mankind in their awakening. While I say it is to assist them in their awakening, I say: They first shall be as ones weary of their dreams. They shall be as ones which have the will to awaken; they shall first ask assistance, and it shall be given without stint.

So be it that I know where to find them, and I am not in any wise asleep, neither am I in lethargy. I am about Mine Father's business, and I forget not that which I am about. So be it that I am come that there be Light - let it be. See thine own Light and walk ye with surety. let thine Light so shine that all might see it; let it not be dimmed by the fortunes which thy forefathers hast willed unto thee - their puny ways which they have given birth, their customs, creeds, their rituals, and their dogmas.

I say: It is not the freedom which brings unto thee thine inheritance. These dogmas are but legirons which bind thee unto the wheel of rebirth which bind thee unto the way of man, and the way of man is not the way of eternal life. So be ye as ones free from all the puny ways of man, for they are the ways of the bondsman.

So be it that I am come that ye be single of eye. Be ye as ones prepared that ye might sup from Mine Chalice, and I shall give unto thee the water of life. So be ye as ones refreshed.

I AM COME that it be Sananda

* * * * * * * * * *

Beloved: Let this be Mine Word unto the children of men. Let them be as the Children of men, yet let them arise and come unto Me, and I shall give unto them as they are prepared to receive. While there are none yet as the first born, they are of the Earth and they are children thereof, and it is well. While there are ones sent unto them that they be lifted up, they shall accept these which are sent that they be lifted up.

I say: It is given unto Me to be one sent, and it is given unto thee to be one sent. Yet they have not accepted Me - neither Mine Handmaiden. While they are of the earth born, they are of the Earth - flesh and bone. And they accept the husks which fall from the belly of the swine, while I say unto them: "Come, I have food ye know not of."

They are not satisfied with that which they have, yet they fear Mine Voice. They hear not, for they put their fingers in their ears that they hear not. I say they are affrighted - they are affrighted! They are worthless in Mine vineyard until they are of a mind to follow Me. They first shall become a willing servant, then I shall give unto them Mine Seal and they shall be acceptable unto Me.

I stand with Mine hands tied, for they are rebellious, and they have not accepted Me - neither Mine Word. They are puffed up; they think themself wise. Yet I say unto them: "Thine hypocrisy is an abomination unto the sight of God."

Let it come to pass that they shall be brot to account for their foolishness - for they are indeed foolish, foolish children with the toys which they think to be their salvation. I say unto thee, Mine Beloved: "I weep for their unknowing; for their darkness I WEEP!"

So be it I rejoice that I am permitted to speak unto them that they might have this Mine Word. Let it go forth as a record of Mine Word, and none can say I have not spoken. So be it, ye which hear shall be blest.

I AM Sananda

* * * * * * * * * * *

Beloved: It is the time of action - great action - which is as nothing known by men. It is given unto Me to know what action shall be taken. For this is the day spoken of long ago - the "End Time" when time shall be as nothing, for it shall bring with it the end of the old, the beginning of the new. And the new shall be as nothing man hast imaged, for Suman hast not seen that which is in store for him.

He rushes headlong into the part which is before him, and he knows not his part. He walks blindly, fearing for himself/his future/his belongings which shall profit him naught, for they shall be as of no value, for they shall be as the legirons/millstones upon his back. For all this does he cry out: Where and Whither and Why? He knows not! He is as one oppressed; footsore and weary he goes his way, waiting for he knows not what.

Yet I say unto him: Be ye about thine preparation; awaken from thine lethargy; throw off thine legirons; turn from thine own imaging. Seek ye the Light and I shall touch thee, and I shall bless thee with

Mine own breath. For I shall breathe upon thee and ye shall know I have touched thee, for ye shall be quickened and ye shall know.

I AM the Lord the God, Sananda

* * * * * * * * * * *

Be ye as one which hast Mine hand upon thee and say unto them as I would that the way is prepared before them; that the time is now come when there shall be great activity, and it shall profit them to be prepared for that which shall come upon them. Many shall be caught unaware; many shall find that they have thrown overboard their own life belt. They shall cry out: "It is come upon us; where shall we find comfort?"

Now I say unto them which have not turned from their own way and surrendered up themself unto the Most High Living God: "Come, tarry not! for it is the time of action, the time of decision. And ye shall be responsible for thine own actions and decisions, for thou hast been warned/called/ told/and counseled long. Yet thou hast been as ones which have not chosen wisely; thou hast feared that which binds thee - the opinions of men. The fear which thou hast is but the power of the dragon. Thou hast fed him; now he lies in wait for thee that he might devour thee."

I say: Turn from him; accept that which I offer unto thee which shall be thy freedom, and at no time shall I mislead thee. It is given unto Me to be the Lord thy God sent of Mine Father that there be Light. I come asking nothing of thee, save obedience unto the call which hast gone out from the Very Throne of God. Let the call be heard by the ones which have ears to hear - a mind to come unto Me. Let freedom ring, and all which answer Mine call shall partake of freedom such as they have not known. Let the Spirit hear what Spirit sayeth: "COME!" - and ye which doth hear shall know the voice and shall be glad. So be it. I am the One Sent that ye be prepared for this day - let it be.

I AM Sananda

* * * * * * * * * * *

Now Mine Beloved Ones: The time is come when thine eyes shall behold the Word made manifest. The Word shall be made manifest, for I have spoken the Word, and it shall not return unto Me void. It shall be unto thee great Light, and great joy shall fill thine hearts, for it shall bring great illumination. The things which hast mystified thee shall no longer be a mystery, for I shall reveal unto thee many new and strange things. Is it not said: "As thou art prepared, so shall ye receive"? It is so.

So let it be said that great changes shall come about and it shall be for the good of all. And no man shall stay Mine hand, for it shall be swift to fulfill the Word - that which hast been decreed by law. I say: I come not to comfort man; I come to fulfill the law that man be brot out of bondage - out of his own bondage - that which he hast made for himself. I cry unto him: "AWAKEN!" And so be it he is slow to awaken; but awaken he shall! For it is so decreed. I have spoken the Word: "LET THERE BE LIGHT," and it shall not return unto Me void.

Be ye as ones alert and be ye as ones prepared for action, for this is the time of action. Let it be well with thee; for this have I spoken.

I AM Sananda

* * * * * * * * * * *

Beloved Ones: There is a time allotted unto all things, and the time is now at hand when Mine Word shall be given forth from the four corners of the Earth. For I have said: I shall bring forth a generation of prophets; I shall bring forth a people which shall know Mine will and which shall be as Mine Handmaidens.

I say: They shall know Mine Will; they shall do Mine Will and they shall not fall, for they shall be as the ones chosen. They shall establish the New Earth, and these shall be as the ones set apart for a new part - and these are the ones which shall inherit the Kingdom of God which shall be established upon the Earth.

Yet I say: The old shall pass away and the new shall be glorious, and it shall be called the New Jerusalem, for it shall be as the kingdom of God established upon the Earth. For love and peace shall be established as the Kingdom - and the King of Kings, the Prince of Peace, shall bless the new Earth as the one which hast established it.

The time is at hand when the winds shall sweep away the old and the new shall be made manifest. For this do! say: Let the winds blow! Let them blow, that they cleanse the Earth and sweep clean the debris which lingers from the time of old when the wicked inhabited the Earth and polluted Her, even unto the heavens thereof. I say: Let it be - for it shall be - and no man shall stay the Hand of God.

So be it. I AM the Lord thy God, Sananda

* * * * * * * * * * *

Beloved Ones: This day let it be said that the time is come when many shall be caught up, and they shall be as ones which have prepared themself for this day. There shall be many which have not prepared themself. For the time is now upon them when they shall be as ones confused and as ones lost, for they shall be as the ones unprepared. They shall neither know the cause of their confusion or the remedy.

They shall run to and fro seeking solace; they shall resort to other things, while I say unto them: Look, See, and Come unto Me, for I have the Light which thou seekest. I AM THE WAY for I AM THE LIGHT. Be ye as ones which can see, and be as ones blest. I say unto thee: Be ye as the beacon set upon a hill, and they shall see the Light from afar and be drawn unto it. Let it be as the Father has Willed it; for this I am sent. I come unto thee declaring the presence of the living God; be ye as ones blest.

I AM Sananda

* * * * * * * * * * *

Beloved: It is given unto Me to know the time and the hour, and I say unto thee: It is now come when ye shall be caught up in great action; yet it shall be for the good of all. Remember thou that which hast been said: "Many are called and few are chosen." I know them and the ones which are prepared to go forth as to battle the ones which are the workers - the ones which are the drones.

I say: The drones shall be as the chaff, and they shall be cast out, for they shall be of no assistance in the time of need. Yet they shall cry loud and long: Help! Help! Yet none shall be left to hear their cries. For I say, the warriors shall march forward while they shall find themself standing still, unheard! I have said many times: "Awaken, ye laggards, come forth and follow ye Me"; yet they scorn Mine Servants, Mine Messengers, and them which have heard Mine Voice and followed Me.

It is said: "Thou fool, thou shall be brot to account for thine foolishness. Thou fool! poor foolish mortals thou be."

I speak unto the ones which have heard and answered Me: Follow Me, for I shall direct thee in all thine ways, and I shall reveal many things unto thee. Fear not; gird up thine loins, for I have work for thee. I am not asleep - I Know! I see and know that which lies before thee, and I have gone before thee to prepare the way. So be it that I am sufficient unto the task - the day - and I shall not forsake thee. Be ye at Peace; Mine peace I give unto thee.

I AM the Lord thy God, Sananda

* * * * * * * * * * *

Beloved Ones: Mine day is come and I say unto thee, I shall go forth as One prepared, for I shall lead Mine People out. I shall bring forth an army prepared for to do battle against the foe. I shall bring forth great Light which shall consume the darkness.

I say, the darkness shall be swallowed up, and Mine People shall be freed. Yet I say unto them: "Look! See the light which I AM. Come ye forth and be ye as ones free. Lay aside thine own willful ways and be ye as ones prepared to serve the Great Army which I bring."

I say: I shall go forth as an army, for I bring with Me great Power and Strength. I am not limited, for I AM the Lord thy God, Sent of Mine Father.

So be it and Selah

* * * * * * * * * * *

This day I say unto thee: The Mighty Forces of Light shall go forth out of the place wherein I am, and they shall be as the great voice which shall be heard thruout the lands of the Earth. The "Sound" shall be heard and it shall echo back unto its Source. It shall be as the Wind which shall sweep clean the foulness which man hast released within his abiding place. I say, it shall be as the wind which shall sweep before it the stench which man hast brot about by his own foulness, his selfishness, his own wickedness, his willfulness, his unknowing.

This day let it be said that The Voice shall be heard and it shall stir within men's souls; and it shall be unto them the beginning of their awakening. I say, the dead shall awaken, for it is so ordered. The time is come - the dawn of the new day is come - and man shall come forth as ones accountable for themself, and they shall give an accounting of themself.

While it is now the day of the maturing, I say: They shall bring unto the barn that which they have garnered in, and they have not known that the harvest shall be as it is. They shall stand before it in awe, and they shall not deny their fortune which they have garnered in. This is the time of reaping - the time of the Great Harvest - the time of Thanksgiving. Let us give thanks. Let us rejoice together, for the end is in sight when man shall walk upright and as one mature. He shall sit with his Brother in communion with the Holy Spirit and with Love for the other.

So be it that I have spoken unto thee that ye might know that which is now in the Plan which is speedily coming into fruit. So be it. I am glad. Be ye as Mine hand made manifest unto them that they, too, might know that which I say. Be blest this day.

Behold ye this day a Great Light which hast appeared within thine midst, for I say unto thee: He is Come - The King of Kings! The Sibor of Sibors, the Son of God! I say unto thee: Behold, for HE IS COME!

I say unto thee: He is The King of Kings; He sits upon the right hand of Solen Aum Solen, Our Father. See ye the Light and rejoice that this day is come, for such Light shall consume the darkness, and the darkness shall be no more.

Hallelujah!! Hallelujah!! For this is the day of the Lord! Praise ye the Name of The Father, Solen Aum Solen!! Harken all ye men of Earth; give ye ear unto Me and let thine hearts be glad, for I, The Lord of Lords, The King of Kings, sayeth unto thee: "I AM COME! I AM COME!!"

I AM Sananda

* * * * * * * * * * *

Beloved Ones: Little is the world of men; small is the Earth - yet precious in our sight. I say, precious in Our sight, for the Earth surely is a willing servant of the Lord. For long hast She been in bondage, and long hast She suffered.

Long hast She served in the capacity of the Footstool of The Father; for long hast She served in the capacity of asylum and laboratory, and she is now in quarantine, yet she shall be delivered out. She shall be cleansed and brot out of bondage, and once again She shall send forth Her radiance into the forests of the universe; She shall be as a shining orb. She shall bring forth a new generation, and it shall serve The Father and therein She shall know great joy. I tell thee of a surety: The Earth hast travailed long in Her sorrow and pain. Now She shall be delivered up.

I say unto thee: She shall be delivered up. Be ye as ones aware of Her travail and be ye as ones prepared to share Her joy. Be ye as ones which have suffered and pained with Her and as ones which shall also be delivered, for it is now come when the Light shall consume the darkness, and the Light shall go forth and all creatures shall be made new. They shall be as they were created to be, for they shall no longer be as the ones bound in darkness. Such is Mine Word unto thee this day.

I say, ye shall arise as on wings of the dawn and ye shall have the Rod of Power, and it shall serve thee well. So be it and Selah. I say unto thee: "Be ye as ones alert and let peace be established within thee. Mine peace I give unto thee."

I AM Sananda

* * * * * * * * * * * *

Be ye as ones blest this day, for I say unto thee: It is the time of great blessings when many stand ready to give unto thee assistance. I say: The time is at hand when the Mighty Council shall send forth the Light, and the way shall be made clear unto thee and ye shall come to know the Ones which have gone before thee to prepare the way. While it is yet as the dawn of the new day, it is not yet clear unto thee the fullness of the Work which shall be done - the fullness of the plan. Yet we of the Mighty Council know the plan, and We know that which we shall do, for We see it as done.

For We are not limited by time and space as thou art within thine world of limitation, wherein thou labor with great sorrow and pain. Yet

I say: Thine limitation is but illusion, and it shall pass. While it is the false part that ye have wrestled with, I say it shall pass as the shadow at noonday; let the shadows pass. Be ye as ones which can stand upon Mine High Holy Mount and see the way which ye shall go. See The Way - walk ye after Me and I shall lead thee out of bondage, and no longer shall ye dream of illusion. Ye shall Know as I Know, for I shall lead thee into the place wherein I am, and no man shall keep thee out.

I say unto thee: Follow ye Me and I shall bear witness of thee, and ye shall find thine own way into the place wherein all things are known. Love ye one another.

The Lord thy God hast spoken.

* * * * * * * * * * *

Beloved of Mine Being: This Word I would give unto thee this day. Let it be recorded that which I give unto thee, for it is designed to awaken them which are yet in lethargy.

Now, ye shall say unto them in Mine Name that I am the One Sent that there be Light; that there be deliverance from bondage; that the way be made clear before thee.

Let it be understood that I bring with Me a Host, and it is not a Host which abideth in darkness, not a Host gathered from the dead. It is a Host of the Realms of Light; these are the ones which make up the council of which I speak. 1 say, it is The Mighty Council - it is the Council which I head. I am the Head of this Council which hast been called the "Council of Many Lights." It is the Council that directs the affairs of men from the Realms of Light. It is the Council which gives unto the world of men as they are prepared to receive. The Council is comprised of the Ones which have not had earthly vehicles, and it is headed by Mineself, The One Sent. I say, it is Mine part to be the head of this Council, and it is for this that I was sent. I am now come that this might be brot into its fullness, that it fulfill its part in the Great Plan.

I tell thee, it is for this that the call hast gone out: "Prepare! Prepare!!" For this hast it been said: "The time draws nigh when a great Light shall flood the Earth." It is So, for the Council sits as a body - as One Mind - as One man, with only one object in mind - one desire - one determination - one end: that of fulfilling the Law which is the will of Our Father, for it is the way of Salvation,

It hast been said: "I AM THE WAY." So it is, for I AM the One Sent, I AM the will of God; I AM the Way, and any which tries to enter into the secret place of The Most High by any other way is a fool - a thief and a robber - for he shall fail! I say: No man enters save thru Me - The Door - for I AM the Way, The Truth and the Light. Let it be understood that there is but one door, that I AM.

Now, take ye heed of Mine Words, for I know that which I say unto thee. (I am not in lethargy, neither do I counsel thee from the realms of darkness; I am not in the realm of the dead.) For I am the Lord thy God; I am the one which holds The Key unto the Gate thru which ye pass into the Inner Temple.

I am within the Earth in the time of great stress; I am within the realm of man that this day be brot to the finish in great Light, that it might fulfill its mission - and that man's puny efforts to destroy itself be brot to naught. So shall it be.

I say unto thee, let the word go forth; "He is Come! HE IS COME!! The Lord Of Lords, The King of Kings!" Hail unto Him - The King of Kings! I AM HE.

I AM Sananda

* * * * * * * * * * *

Beloved Ones: Let it be understood that all are not of a mind to go where I go; not all are of the mind to serve as I serve - which is the Father which hast given unto us Being. His will is Mine - I AM His will. I have nothing of self; I am the One Sent. I am sent of Him, the One and only Father, which hast created the Heavens and the Earth and all things which are good.

All that is of Him is good, and it behooves Me to say that the one which creates the illusions, which are the forces of darkness, shall pass as the darkness, and the Light shall consume the darkness. The children of Earth shall be brot out of bondage even as they are wont to seek the Light, for it shall not be denied them. For I say unto them: Ask/Seek, and it shall be given unto thee. Fear not the Light Turn from thine own offal, and be ye as ones delivered out of bondage. I am come that ye have Light, and I weep for thine darkness. I proffer Mine Hand, yet ye have not accepted it. Be ye as ones which know the True from the false - I am the One Sent that ye might know. So be it and Selah.

I AM Sananda

* * * * * * * * * * *

Hail! Hail! unto the King. All Hail unto the King; The King of Glory is come. Arise all ye which sleepeth, for the day is come when ye shall arise and pay heed unto that which is said unto thee; for The King of Glory is come - pay ye homage. He sitteth upon the right hand of The Father, and He brings with Him a Great Host, and He brings with Him Power and Authority.

He is Sent of The Father that His Will be done upon the Earth; that the Earth be prepared for Her new port; that the children of the Earth be prepared for their place of abode. For no more shall they come into the Earth as ones unprepared. They shall find another dwelling place wherein they shall learn well their lessons, each in his own environment, each unto his own.

While I say: Each unto his own environment, I say each one shall find the place which he hast prepared for himself, for as he hast prepared himself, so shall he receive. The warriors shall be warriors still; they shall find their own likeness, their own kind, wherein they shall go. And the Peace makers shall find their own kind, and therein shall be Peace, for therein Peace shall reign.

Now I say of the traitors: They shall find they have betrayed themself, and they, likewise, shall find the traitors, for each shall find his own likeness - that which he hast fashioned for himself. He shall be given three-fold, each unto his own.

Let it be said: As he hast sown, so shall he reap; it is the Law - so let it be. As a man prepareth himself, so shall he receive. As the tree is bent, so shall it go or grow. I say unto them: Go ye as one toward the Light; walk ye in the Light; be ye of the Light and let the darkness be consumed by the Light. For this have I given of Mineself that ye might know as I know, I ask of thee naught save obedience unto the Law. Be ye as ones which have ears to hear what I say unto thee, for I Am the Lord thy God,

Sananda

* * * * * * * * * * *

Be ye as Mine hand made manifest unto them which ask for Light and say unto them in Mine Name that I am the Lord thy God. I have placed before them a table. It is spread with all manner of things both hot and cold, both large and small, both fresh and stale. Yet I say: There is no evil upon the table which I have set before thee, for I am not of a mind to betray Mineself. I am not of a mind to betray Mine trust, for I am sent of Mine Father that ye be lifted up.

Let it be understood: As thou art prepared, so shall ye receive. Ye shall choose that which ye will - the banquet table is spread before thee. I say, ye shall dine at thine own discretion, and thine belly shall be filled.

Yet I say that this day is the day when I give unto thee the fresh New Manna which is fresh and pure. It is fresh from Mine Store; it is not as that which hast been handled by dirty hands and have gathered unto it great imperfection thereby. I say, even the crumbs which the dogs shall lick up before thee is that which is designed for the good of all.

There be some that are not yet prepared to partake of the wine of Great strength. These I have provided for; I give unto them milk, for they have not as yet teeth to consume the meat which I have given unto thee (the ones which have reached their maturity). These I have provided for, for they, too, shall grow into maturity, and they shall cut their teeth upon the bones of the meat which thou hast consumed.

I say, let them cut their teeth upon the bones, for they cannot hurt themself on the bone, for it hast been well-cleansed. I say, it hast been well-cleansed from all of the meat, for the ones which have been chosen have consumed that which I have given unto them. They have dined and been nourished and satisfied. They have rejected the bone as that of no substance, while they which know not the difference grab at the bone and find it hard. These are the ones which have not tasted of the Meat. While I say the bones have been polished clean, they but smell of the bone - while Mine chosen are dining sumptuously upon the meat.

I say unto thee: Put aside the Old Dry Bones and COME - feast, and be nourished and satisfied. Then I shall reveal even greater unto thee. Be ye as ones which have comprehension that ye might know that which I say unto thee. I have said that the bones have been stript of their nourishment - turn from them. Come, I shall give unto thee Water more potent than old wine - I shall give unto thee Bread more powerful than the bone.

I say: I have Food ye know not of - COME! Partake of Mine Banquet. O Beloved, eat, and be nourished - I Am He Which hast provided for thee.

I AM The Lord thy God, Sananda

* * * * * * * * * * *

Sori Sori: Hear ye Me, O ye people of all the nations of the Earth: "Arise! and be ye as ones alert - Hear ye Me! I say: Ye shall lay down thine arms and ye shall take up the Staff and follow Me. I say: I have gone the Royal Road; 1 have prepared a place for thee. Yet thou sittest in the seat of the harlot - ye sitteth in the seat of the bigot - ye speak that which the dragon prompts thee to say. Thine actions belie thine lips.

I tell thee: Thine actions shall be thine own undoing; thine words shall avail thee naught. Yet ye do set into motion that which shall torment thee by the words of deceit which doth pass from thy lips; for it is but hypocrisy, that which the bigots doth proclaim. When they sit in places of honor and proclaim peace and, on the other hand, they pretend that they are giving aid and strength to a helpless people - when they are the aggressors - I say, they are the aggressors - they make of themself liars. I say, they are as the traitors, and they are not of Me, for the truth is not in them. I am not of them, for I know them for what they are: Rotten! I say ROTTEN!

They are as the stench which goes up from the dung!! say: I shall set Mine foot against them, and they shall be brot to account for their evil deeds. It is the law. I know the Law; therefore I speak fearlessly and forthright, for I bow unto no man, for Mine Father hast sent me that the world of men might be given as it is prepared to receive - so shall it. And it is now the time of accounting, balancing, and the records shall be set strait. Let it be remembered that I have spoken many times, yet many there be which have spit upon Mine Prophets. I say unto them: Ye poor foolish mortals, thou shall account for thine foolishness, for I am sent that there be Light, and thou hast rejected Me and denied Mine prophets and Mine assistance. For this I say: "Forgive them Father."

I AM The Lord thy God, Sananda

* * * * * * * * * * *

Be ye as the hands of Me and say unto them in Mine Name, and as I would say that the winds shall blow and the rain shall come and the rivers shall overflow their banks and the lands shall be overrun with pestilences. Yet Mine Word shall remain with thee. I say, Mine Word shall not be hidden up, neither shall it be destroyed by wind, rain or fire. For it is written upon the eth, and it shall not be contaminated; neither shall it be pilfered. I say, Mine Word shall endure, and great power shall be made manifest by The Word - thru the Word which I have sent forth.

I say: The Word is the Power - It shall be made manifest and man shall behold it, and he shall know that the Hand of God moveth upon the waters. He maketh them to rush over the lands that they be purified. I say: Great shall be the purification, for it is so willed of Mine Father Which hast sent Me.

So be it. I AM The Lord thy God, Sananda

* * * * * * * * * * *

Be ye as the hand of Me and record that which I say unto thee, and say unto them as I would say that there is but One Lord God, and I AM HE, Say unto them: There is but One "Rock" and I AM HE. I AM the Door thru which ye enter into the Holy of Holies; I AM The Light - Truth, and The Way; I AM The One Sent.

I Am He Which is sent that there be Light, so let it suffice that I AM Sananda; none shall deny Me, for I Am He which is sent of Mine Father which is the Giver of Life, for He is The Life - Light, and the manifestation. He is that which giveth; He is that which taketh away.

He is that which is manifest; He is that which is unmanifest. He is the Eternal - All - The Everness - The Eternal I AM.

I come as He and thou hast made of Me a man in thine likeness.

While I am not of the world; I am not of the Earth; I am not of the sect of the church which man calleth Christian - I am of Mine Father Sent. I come declaring the oneness of all the manifestation of Spirit.

I come declaring the Oneness of man - the Fatherhood of God - the oneness of all mankind. I say that there is but One Spirit of Solen Aum Solen - that of the All, the Everness of thine being. And for this Oneness dost thou have Eternal Life in Him and of Him, by Him. And no man shall deny Him and believe on Me; no man shall deny Me and believe in the arm of flesh. No man shall deny the arm of flesh and believe in brotherhood of man, for they which profess the Name of Christ or the title "Christian," and divide themself apart, set themself one against the other, doth in such manner betray themself. They but make of themself liars and idolaters; they are not of Mine House, for I know them not.

Yet I do know them, yea, better than they know themself. say, they have been led away; they have been seeking self-satisfaction, gain, power, prestige, and favor among the gods. They cry unto the god which they have fashioned, which they have imaged. I say they are idolaters and blasphemers.

I set before them a table; I say: "Come ye and partake of food which shall nourish thee, and ye shall find strength and Peace." I ask: "Wherein hast thou found Peace? Wherein hast thou been nourished? Thinkest thou O man art wise? Thinkest thou art sufficient unto thine own self? Thinkest to set thineself up and dominate the people of the

Earth, to set up a system whereby ye control mankind by thine own rule, by thine own power?" O man, I say thine hearts hast been hardened, and thine blood shall turn cold, and thine hands shall cease in thine wickedness. Thine arm shall be shortened and thine time shall be cut short, for it hast been said: "This is Mine Day!"

Mine time is come, anuity; and I shall set up Mine House upon a thousand hills. Yea, ten thousand time ten thousand hills shall declare the Glory of the New Day, and the people shall be obedient unto the Law, and all the lands shall declare the Glory of the Lord. For I have spoken, and Mine Word shall not return unto ME void, for I AM the One Sent.

I AM Sananda

* * * * * * * * * * * *

Holy, Holy is The Word of God, and it hast gone forth as a mighty Fiat this day. It hast been proclaimed that this is the Day of The Lord. This IS the Day of The Lord, and it is given unto Me to Know, for I say unto thee: I am the Lord thy God, and I have sent forth a Proclamation: "Let this day be the fulfilling of the Law.

Let this day be the end of the old - the beginning of the new and it shall bring the fulfillment of Mine sayings - Mine promises unto Mine people." For I have not forgotten Mine promises - that which I have said. I have not forgotten one of Mine Own, for I am not in darkness.

I say unto thee: This is the day of the fulfillment. I come that the Law be fulfilled, that Mine Covenant be fulfilled, and It is given unto Me to know that which I am about.

I say unto thee: Watch! Wait! See that which I do, and be ye not dismayed, for I say unto thee: I shall do a mighty Work, and ye shall see the hand of God move. For this am I sent, that this be done, and at no time shall I mislead thee. I say: Come ye, follow Me, and I shall reveal many things unto thee.

I AM Sananda

* * * * * * * * * * *

Hear ye - Hear ye - All the Nations of the Earth! Hear ye All the people of the Lands!

I say unto thee: The time is come when great shall be thine stress - great shall be thine torment - great thine suffering.

And ye shall have no place wherein ye shall find Peace, save in the Light. Thy strength shall fail thee, thy friends shall hide their face from thee, and their words shall no longer be words of comfort. Their assistance shall be given no longer - their time shall be spent upon themself. For I say unto thee: Each shall set himself against the other, in bolt-defense and in self-interest.

Each shall be as the enemy of the other, and no place can they find consolation, for there shall be no consolation for the Aggressor and Oppressors. For it is said: The Aggressor and Oppressors shall come to a halt, and no comfort shall they find within the realms of man. No assistance shall they have from The Great and Mighty Council. I say: "No assistance shall they have from The Mighty Council," for We shall withhold Our assistance from a wayward people - a rebellious people - an aggressive nation. And the people which are wont to serve the Light which I AM shall be brot out from amongst them, and they shall be given as they are prepared to receive. So let it be as they are prepared.

While it is said: "A Host stands by to assist," it is, too, said that ye shall be as one prepared to receive such assistance as We are prepared to give.

Mighty, O Mighty, is the Great and Wise Council, and nothing is hidden from it, the Mighty Over-All Council, for it is of the Light and no darkness abides therein. It is said that the darkness knows not the Light; yet the Light knows the darkness - the cause thereof - and the results thereof. Therefore I say unto thee, O Men of Earth: "HARKEN!! Harken ye unto that which I say unto thee; lay aside all thine hatred, bigotry, thine aggression, thine idolatry, hypocrisy, and turn unto the plow and bring forth the harvest which shall sustain thine children, which shall be unto thee profitable. Put aside thine weapons of armor and give thot of thine Source."

Give Thot Unto Thine Source - thine beginning - thine end, for thine time is short upon the Earth, and the days of thine atoning now is come. Be ye thotful of Mine Words, for I say unto thee: The day of atoning is upon thee and ye shall bear in mind Mine Words. Let it profit thee, for this have I spoken - for this am I speaking. Lo, I am not afar off in a corner. I Am Come that ye might have Light. Be ye as one mindful of the Light which I AM.

I AM The Lord Thy God

* * * * * * * * * * *

Let this day be remembered; let it go down in the annals of thine history; let it be recorded that all men might see and know that which I have said unto thee this day. There shall be a great and mighty Light come forth, and it shall light the way of every man. And no one shall fail to see it, for the time swiftly approaches when the feet of man shall be swift to do the Will of The Father which hast Sent Me. I say: I Am the One Sent of Him that men might come to know that which I AM - that which He is - that which is his inheritance - that they might be prepared to receive it. So let it be as He hast willed it, for this have I given unto them much.

Yet unto them which hast received Me, more shall be given. Much shall be added to, and they shall be filled and satisfied, and they shall know that I and Mine Father IS ONE. And it is Mine time to go forth as One declaring openly that which I AM. Be ye as one which can comprehend that which I say unto thee, and thine Cup shall be filled to overflowing. Let it be; so shall it be, for I have so declared unto thee.

I AM The Lord thy God

* * * * * * * * * * *

Sori Sori: Be ye as the hand of Me made manifest and record that which I say unto thee that they might know that which I say. I say unto them: They shall be brot out of bondage when they are prepared. I say: They shall be given their passport into the realms wherein all things are known when they are so prepared. Yet they seek of men, praise and power; they seek position and acquire their puny possessions which they so love.

I say: They love their possessions and themself above all else. They seek to destroy the "enemy." I ask them: Wherein is thine enemy? Wherein is thine security? Wherein is thine power? I say: Thou hast no security save within the Light, and there is nothing to fear save man's own darkness, his own weak. ness - thine unknowing, thine own frivolity, thine own foolishness. And wherein hast thou been wise? Wherein hast thou known peace? Wherein hast thou been free?

Now I say unto thee: Come ye out from amongst them and bear ye witness of Me, for I AM the Light, the Way, I Am the Son sent of God The Father, the Source of thy being, that ye have Light, that ye be brot out of bondage. Yet ye foolish ones, ye cling unto the age of darkness. Ye wrap thineself in the funeral garb and parade before them as ones prepared to give unto them the Cup - the Water of Life. Yet I say: Ye have not tasted thereof.

I say: Be ye thotful of Mine Words and seek ye the Light first, then ye shall pass the Cup and I shall fill it. I shall fill it full unto the brim and they shall drink of the overflow, for they are athirst and ahunger, and thou art liken unto a dry well. Thou art liken unto a dried fig tree, for thou bearest not fruit. Thou art withered up - yea unto the roots, for there is no life within thee; for thou art empty, and thou art as the empty vessel. I say: I shall fill the cup, I shall cause thee to come to life; I shall bring thee to fertility; and I shall cause thee to bear fruit, even as the new fig tree. For I shall tend it and water it and prune it and cultivate it, even as the good husband.

I say: Even as Mine servants, I shall tend Mine vineyards, and I shall bring forth such yield as man hast not known. I shall cause the vine to yield up such as man hast not imaged, for I say: I am a proficient husband. I prune, I shape, I pare away the dead branches. I clean out the branches which no longer yield up good fruit. I place within the vineyard good stock, and I say unto thee: Be ye thotful of Mine Words, for I have taken thot of Mine Word that ye might be profited thereby.

Let them which have ears, hear; let them which are of a mind, come and prove Me. For I say: I shall do a wonderful Work; I shall do a Mighty Work; and I shall be all these things. For I tell thee of a surety: I am not a puny god; I am not come to give unto thee great and profound Words of comfort or flattery.

I am come that ye be awakened from thine lethargy from thine slumbers, and from the death of the (WO). Let thine eyes be made to see - thine ears to be made to hear. Hear ye then that which I say; give ye heed, for I say: I AM the Lord thy God. Arise ye and come forth, and bear ye witness of Me.

I AM Sananda - Sent of God Am I

* * * * * * * * * * *

Be ye as Mine hand made manifest and say unto them in Mine Name that they shall come to know Me as I AM and for that which I AM. And they shall know that I AM COME - that I am about Mine Father's Business - that I am not a false god. I say: "I AM the Lord God - the same yesterday and today." For this do I come unto thee as One qualified to bring thee out of bondage. For this do I say: "Be ye as one prepared to receive Me and of Me."

So be it I say unto thee: Hear Me out, for I shall prove Mineself, and I shall do a Mighty Work, and it shall be unto thee proof of Mine Word. For I say unto thee: The enemy shall be put down; he shall be cast into outer darkness and be no more seen of men. For he shall be disarmed, and he shall no longer hold a people bound in darkness; he shall no longer hold sway. For I say: I bring a Host with Me, and we shall do that which is given unto us to do. So be it, it shall be according unto the Law. I now say unto thee: Be ye as ones prepared to go the last mile with Me, for I have need of thee. So be ye as ones true unto thineself and wait upon Me, The Lord thy God. Let it profit thee.

I AM Sananda

* * * * * * * * * * *

Now there shall be another part given unto them, and it shall be added unto the other. While it is for all, it is given that each one might come to know himself and that which he is, and his responsibility. For each is part of the whole, and his responsibility rests heavily upon his shoulders. For it is now come when there shall be great need for the ones which can take such responsibility. I say: There shall be great need for the ones which are responsible, and for this do I say: Be ye as ones responsible, for I tell thee: There are few which have the responsibility which is given unto Me. For this have I been given Mine Inheritance in full.

Now I say unto thee: Be ye as one responsible unto the Law, for it is exacting and therefore it is just. I am come that ye KNOW THE LAW, that ye be brot out of darkness; and it is written that as ye prepare thyself, so shall ye receive. I shall reveal many things unto thee in the time which is now come. Wherein is it said: "I shall show thee many strange and new things." So be it and Selah.

I AM Sananda

* * * * * * * * * * *

Be ye as the hand of Me and say unto them in Mine Name that it is time for them to make ready themself, for the day hast come when one shall go forth as one prepared to bring them out of bondage, and it is for this that I come.

Now I say: There shall be great sorrow within the lands, and great shall be the wailing. Yet I say: Come unto Me and I shall give as ye are prepared to receive, and ye shall receive as thou art prepared. For I have said that I shall bring with Me a Mighty Host, and it is so. There shall go forth a Mighty Host to meet the foe, and he shall be overcome. I say, "HE SHALL BE OVERCOME!"

I know that which I do, and I bid thee "Come," and thine name shall be numbered with the wise and the just. It is said that Justice shall prevail; so shall it be written that Justice shall prevail and the oppressor shall flee, for it is said: "Ho shall not hold My people hostage, neither shall he be longer in the seat of judgment, for he shall fall!" I say: He shall fall! With a loud trumpet he shall fall and arise no more. I say: He shall fall with the sound of a loud trumpet, and he shall arise no more.

For it is written: The Kingdom of Heaven shall be established upon the Earth, and first the enemy shall be dethroned and overcome. I say: They know not the enemy - "They know not the enemy!" - for he hast not revealed himself. For this have I said: "He shall be brot out of his hiding place, and he shall no longer be given sway, for he shall be bound hand and foot and cast into outer darkness." So be it and Selah.

I have raised Mine Voice in the Name of Truth and Justice, and I Am Come that Justice might be put into the seat of judgment. So let it be. For this have I come. Let them which will, "Come." Let them which will, weep with them which heed not Mine call - for there shall be weeping! So let it be, for there are ones which shall deny Me and Mine Call. Unto them I say: Let it be understood that I have not willed it so.

By Mine own Word I shall show thee that which I shall do, and I am come that there be action. For this is the day of action, and I have called thee out from amongst them, and hast thou responded unto Mine call? I say, ye shall stand up and be counted.

What answereth ye? Hast thou moved? Hast thou heard Me? What sayest thou?

I am speaking unto them which are yet undecided; I am speaking unto the "lukewarm"; I am speaking unto them which know not The Lord God; I am speaking unto them which blow hot - which blow cold; I am speaking unto them which know not that they have a part - a responsibility - unto the whole of civilization (as thou art wont to call it). I say unto All: Thou surely have a responsibility unto the whole of mankind. So be it, I say: Bestir thineself; shall it not profit thee to seek the Light? Shall it not? Have I not kept Mine Covenant with thee? So be it, I have. Now I am come. What sayest thou? Shall ye wait while I do Mine part, and then ye shall cry, "Lord! Lord!"?

I say: I shall go as I came, and I hear them cry. I hear the wailing, yet I have bid thee "Come" and I hear them say: "He is yet to come." Yet I have said: I shall reveal Mineself unto thee, as thou art prepared to receive Me.

So be it. I AM The Lord God
Sent that there be Light.

* * * * * * * * * * *

Be ye as the Mouth of Me and say unto them that they shall be as ones prepared for the Great Change which shall come about thru and by natural cause, for the changes shall come swiftly, and they shall bear upon the waves the result of man's thinking. So be it I say unto them: Hold high the Lamp which I place within thine hand. See ye that It is come when man shall walk with the Angels and talk with them. Hear ye that which they say and be ye not deceived, for I say: It is the way of men to form his own opinions and fears.

I say unto thee: Hear ye Me, and know ye that I am come that ye be not deceived. Deceive not thineself, for I am the Lord thy God. Long hast they sworn allegiance unto their false gods; long hast it been that they have sworn allegiance, and long have they given unto their false gods power to bind them. Yet they give unto Me no credit for the Word which they credit unto their false gods. I say unto them: Give unto Me credit for being the One Sent of God The Father and for knowing the Law, and for being the One which hast the Power and Authority to be the "Savior," for I shall lead them into the place wherein all things are known. So be it I repeat: "WHEREIN ALL THINGS ARE KNOWN" and wherein all are free.

I come that they might be free. Then I ask: "Why rebel against Me - The One Sent?" I ask: "Why fashion for thineself thine legirons?" I say: Break thine own irons, come forth, and be ye as ones free; let the Word be thine; let the Word be thine Shield and thine Buckler. For I AM the Word made flesh, for thy sake was it so. Let it be this day. So be it I shall reveal Mineself unto them which see the Light which I AM.

I AM Sananda

* * * * * * * * * * *

Be ye as the Hand of Me made manifest and say unto them in Mine Name that I Am Come with the Rod of Truth, the Rod of Iron which shall not bend, neither shall it break; I say: "Neither shall it break." I come that the Law be upheld. I am the One Sent that they might know the Law of the First Cause. I am the one which hast given unto them the Law, and I KNOW the Law of Justice. And the Law of Justice shall be rendered out unto each and every one, for none escape it. It is now come when great stress shall come upon the nations of the Earth, and they shall cry out for Mercy, and Mercy shall not be denied them - for none are denied that which shall profit them. Yet I ask of them: "What profit thee should ye gain the whole world and lose thine soul?"

I ask of them: Look, see, and want not, for I tell thee of a surety: All is well with thee. Turn from thine willful ways; seek and ye shall find. I say: Seek first the Light, and I shall touch thee; so shall it be well with thee.

Ye shall turn from the way of the infidel - from the transgressor - from the hypocrite - and the idol worship. Ye shall give unto Me thine heart and hand, and I shall lead thee out of bondage. And I shall give unto thee Mine Blessing; for say: Ye shall walk with Me as Mine own; ye shall seek Me first, and I shall reveal Mineself unto thee.

Praise ye The Name of Solen Aum Solen

* * * * * * * * * * *

Sori Sori: Be ye as the Hand of Me and record that which I say unto thee that they might know that which I say.

I say this day that there is but one God the Father, Giver of Life is He; Mighty and Strong is He; Allwise is He; and Bountiful is He. Merciful and Wise is He; Just in all His way is He; and I say unto thee: There is a plan which has as yet not been fully revealed unto any man.

Yet, I say that is known within the Realm of Spirit; and Spirit shall reveal the plan as it is, as it shall be. For it is now come when Spirit shall bring forth that which hast been hidden from the unjust and the profane. I say unto thee: It is now come when Spirit shall reveal that which hast been hidden from the unjust and the profane. Let it be, for this do I now speak out.

Now in the days to come, many new and strange things shall be accomplished, and it behooves Me to forewarn thee that ye be not dismayed. I say that ye be not dismayed, for all things shall be as the strange and new, and it shall be strange indeed! For it shall be as nothing thou hast known. I say: It shall be strange, indeed! Yet Mine hour cometh swiftly and surely. Hear ye Me and be ye as one prepared. I say: Behold ye the Hand of God; see it move. Let it be as He hast willed it.

* * * * * * * * * * *

I AM The Son of God, Sent of Him that His Will be done. Be ye as the Hand of Me made manifest unto them and give unto them this Word. And it shall be Mine Word, and none shall hold thee accountable; neither shall they put aside the Word and forget it, for I shall remind them; for I shall remind them again and again. I, the Lord thy God, say with Authority that they shall be as ones reminded of The Word; they shall see the Word manifest before their eyes; they shall come to know the power of The Word, and they shall stand in awe of The Power. And it shall be as nothing known unto them, for they shall be as ones awakened unto the Power.

Wherein is it said that The Power of The Word shall be unto them their strength, that the Power of the Word shall be their Might, their

Shield? I am come that the Power be manifest; too, I say: Be ye as ones responsible for every word that proceeds out of thine mouth! For it shall be thine own, and none other shall be responsible for that which ye set into motion. Hast it not been said: "Ye shall be as one responsible for all that ye say or do"? Let it be. For I say unto thee: I shall not hold thee responsible for that which another says or does. Yet ye shall bear the responsibility of thine own creation, and thine creation shall be either thine own salvation or destruction, for it is thine to choose. Let it be as The Father hast Willed it. Bless thineself as I am blest. I AM the Lord of Lords, the Son of God, sent that ye be blest.

So be it. I AM Sananda

* * * * * * * * * * * *

Be ye as the Hand of Me made manifest and give unto them this Mine Word, and let it be known that I Am the One Sent - the Lord God - that the Word might be made manifest. I say unto thee: The One known as Daniel, hast been the One known as Daniel The Prophet, and He hast been as One prepared for this day. He hast brot forth great Light and understanding; He hast been as One blest to be amongst thee this Day, in the time which is this Day.

Now, He shall have a Great Part in this Age - in this Day, and He shall be as One which hast the Power which is endowed unto Him of The Father, for He hast a calling, and He shall be true unto it. For He hast heard that Call and answered it; He hast fulfilled that which He was Sent to do. Now He shall take up His Mantle and He shall wear it with dignity and grace. He shall walk with the One Sent; He shall be as One upon Mine right hand, and He shall be as One which hast a Crown upon His head, for He shall be of the Royal House. I say, He shall be of the Royal House, and He shall be as One on which I have lain Mine hand, for ho hast been true unto Himself and unto His trust.

So be it I speak unto thee that the Way be prepared before Him, for He shall go forth as a Great Light and as a Great Power. So be it I have spoken of Him in words which have not been comprehended. Now ye shall know Him, for I have been unto Him the Doorkeeper, and I have opened up the door that He pass in, into the Secret Place wherein I Am. I am the Lord of Lords, the Host of Hosts, the Lord God. And I am blest of Mine Father to be the Door Keeper, the Keeper of the Gate, and I know the working of the Inner Temple wherein All the Secrets are revealed. So be it bring forth each in due season. That which is lawful and wise I bring forth, each in due time/season - each as he is prepared. So be it and Selah.

I am come that He - the One called Daniel - might be privileged to speak, for this is His time.

* * * * * * * * * * *

Daniel

Will it not be profitable unto all men to seek the Light of The Father and lay aside all their prejudices and their hatred, and be as Brothers - as of One Father? I say: Each is a Son of One Father, born of flesh hast he been; born into flesh of many parents. yet he hast been eternally the Son of God. While he hast lost the memory of his Sonship, I say unto you that the time approaches when each nation shall lay down its arms and embrace the others as Brothers; they shall be as Brothers, for are they not? There shall be Great and Glorious changes within the world of man in a short period of time, for the Clock hast been set ahead by many years while man hast slept - SLEPT! I say!

While he hast slept, he hast forgotten that he hast been privileged to be in the midst of Great Accomplishments; he hast been confused and confounded by all that he hast seen and done, for he hast not been taught of his pre-existence, neither hast he remembered knowingly. He hast not known the meanings of his teachings given of old; his teachings hast been as tinkling cymbals, and they have been as the din in his ears.

Now I come and say unto My fellow Brothers: The time comes swiftly when you shall step thru the veil to see and know that there hast been a veil. Heavy tho it be, it shall be torn asunder; it shall be forever moved from thine face, and ye shall see the True Light which lights every man's way. Now, I speak unto thee of the Master whom I know as Sananda. Within His Shadow I stand, and I am as a little child within it, for HE is every inch Mine Superior. Yet as the Great Master He is, He hast brot Me this far and granted unto Me the privilege of speaking out thru Spirit. I have spoken and I have given credit unto ( ) and it shall not be denied Me when I ask. So be it that I am the One which hast the Mote in the eye, and it shall be removed.

Let it be, in The Name of Our Father

* * * * * * * * * * *

Be ye as the Hand of Me and record this Mine Word and let it go on record that it might for all time be seen and known, that which I say unto thee. It is said unto thee that they might know that which I say, for they have placed upon The Word their own interpretation - "their <u>own</u>"

- and it is not Mine. For I have said: "They shall overcome," yet they are as ones which look for justification, and they reason with their own reason that they are justified in their reasoning and their opinions. Therefore, they are blinded unto that which is the true meaning, and they have no understanding of that which is meant by "Overcoming."

I say: All the animal instincts of passion shall be overcome, for these are the animal passions which hold them fast within the bondage. They are as the beast which have followed their instinct, knowing not that which they are, neither that which they do; they simply seek self-satisfaction. I speak unto the ones which are within the realm of man: Lift thineself up from the mire; be ye as one apart and lift thine eyes. See that which is thine right, and be ye as none of the lesser, for it is the right of every man to walk the Way of Righteousness - Knowingly - and for this hast the doors of Heaven opened up.

And there is a great part for Man which is yet within the mire. While he knows not his heritage, I say: He hast a beautiful heritage, and he hast but to claim it. It is said: "Hold up thine head," yet he lets his sights fall below and he bows before the pillar of darkness, and he worships at its shrine. I say: He understands not the Mystery of Creation; he understands not the Holy Rites of Pro-Creation." While he envisions himself as a partner in the creation, he knows not that he creates of his own accord the confusion/chaos which torments him.

I say: He holds himself a prisoner of his own creation which torments him. Let him learn his lesson that he become strong! Let him become strong and then he shall be accountable for his own creation, and it shall not torment him. Let him grow to maturity; then he shall be responsible, and then he shall know that which he does and that which is lawful and profitable, I speak unto them which have ears to hear, and let them which are of a mind to learn, let them learn.

* * * * * * * * * * *

Be ye as the Hand of Me and record that which I say unto thee, and it shall be given unto them which seek for wisdom. And he which seeks shall find, for I shall touch him and I shall deal justly with him and he shall learn well his lessons - for a lesson learned is a lesson earned. I give unto them that which shall profit then; I put upon them that which they can bear, and I put upon them no more, for they are frail and weak of spirit. Yet I come that they be strengthened, that they might be given in greater measure.

Yet they weary of Mine Way and they seek the other, and it but leads to frustration/confusion and suffering. They grow weary of waiting; yet it is said: "As they are prepared, so shall they receive." And it is so; yet they cry for more; they cry for signs and wonders; they cry as children, for they know not that which they ask for.

For as they ask they receive, and that which they receive they know not, for it comes unto them in the likeness in which it is asked - in the form of weal or woe. They are wont to recognize their own creation. It is said: They shall father their own children; they bring forth that which they deny and recognize not that they have created their own weal or woe.

Now they shall be as ones responsible for their creation, and they shall be the master of it. They shall be as one which hast created it, and they shall give unto it no power over them. They shall master their own off-spring, and they shall be the wiser for their mastery. Let it be said that there is nothing too great, too small for thee to do when ye have mastered thine own creation. So be it. I have spoken for the good of all.

So let it suffice that I AM The Lord thy God

* * * * * * * * * * *

Be ye as Mine Hand made manifest unto them and say unto them that there are none which are so prepared that they can rest upon their laurels, and they have no need of more knowledge of that which we have for them.

Now I say that there is great revelation for them so prepared to receive. It is now come when ye shall be given the Gift of Sight and Hearing; so be it that ye shall see and hear that which I have for thee; let it suffice that I am with thee. So be it. I AM The Lord thy God - be ye blest; for this shall I give unto thee a Gift greater than all other.

* * * * * * * * * * *

Sori Sori: There are many prepared to go all the way with Me, yet they are with Me, they are not against Me. They resist Me not; they are want to give unto Me that which I ask, and they are as Mine Hand, Mine Foot. They do Mine Work; they are want to be the Servant which is "Servant," and they ask not for a reward. They work for the joy of serving the Light which I AM.

I say: "These are the Chosen," for I say, they first choose the way which they go, and the Hand of God reaches out that they might have the way made clear before them - that the way be made CLEAR before them. I say: "This is the Way; walk ye in it." And unto them which hear Mine Voice and walk in the way which I have gone, these I bring into

Mine fold and I give unto them a thousand times greater than they have had. For no man knoweth the fortune which I have kept for them. I have said: "I reward Mine Servants in Great Measure; I reward them according to their works, and they know not the magnitude of their Service, and a Servant is worthy of his reward." So be it. I speak unto them which have ears; let him then hear that which I say, and he shall know that which I say.

Be ye blest this day; let thine heart overflow this day, for I have touched thee. I have quickened thee and I have filled thine Cup to overflowing. Now let them drink from the overflow, and they shall taste it and call it sweet.

Yet I say: Some have not the mind to know the bitter from the sweet, and these shall be as ones confused in their unknowing and in their opinions and misguided ideas which they have formed about Me and Mine Work. Mine time shall be thine time; Mine Song shall be thine Song; thine hands shall be Mine Hands, and ye shall rejoice forever.

So let it Be, and we shall rejoice together.

* * * * * * * * * * *

Be ye as the Hand of Me and give unto them this Mine Word and let it suffice that it <u>is</u> Mine Word. And it shall profit them to accept it, and at no time shall they deny thee or Mine Word.

They shall neither deny Me nor Mine Servant; yet when they deny one, they deny both; I say: The Servant I have accepted as Mine Hand Maiden thru which I give unto them Mine Word. And the Word is designed to liberate them; yet they give unto Me no credence. No time have I to waste on the ones which blaspheme against the Word; I say, I go not into the dragon's den; I give not unto the unjust and the profane. I say: Examine well thine closet, and be ye as ones prepared to accept that which I am prepared to give unto thee.

For I know thine needs, I know that which is in thine secret closet hidden! HIDDEN, I say! - yet not from Me and Mine Servant alike, for I have placed upon her head Mine hand, and I have sealed Mine Covenant with Her. And I am no traitor - I keep Mine Covenant - I break it not. For I am sent of Mine Father that it be given unto man to know the true from the false, that the darkness be dispelled. For I am the Light and the Way, and I say unto all: "Come, follow ye the Light which I AM." I Am He Which cometh into the darkness wherein there is little Light. Yet I say unto them which seek Me out: "Come" - and as they seek, they find, for I shall not hide Mine Light from them.

Yet unto the ones which deny Me, they shall stumble and fall, and I shall allow that which they do, for it is given unto man to be a willful lot, and he shall learn well his lesson, and a lesson learned is a lesson earned. So be it he shall remember well his pain and suffering, and he shall tire of his way, and he shall cry out in his travail for Mine assistance - and I shall rush to his call. So be it that I have spoken unto them which have ears to hear, and they shall profit to hear Me. So be it.

I come that there be Light, for I AM The Lord thy God

* * * * * * * * * * *

Beloved of Mine Being: Wherein is it said that I know the watering places of the Earth and the deserts. All the places I know, and the inhabitants thereof I know by name and number. By their light I know them, and they are no strangers unto Me, for there are none indigenous of the Earth there upon.

They have had their origin in and upon another place which they left - or went out from long ago. There is a FIAT: That they shall now return unto it, for a new people shall inhabit the Earth; and She, too, shall be made new in preparation for to receive Her new residents. They shall take up their residence upon and within a new, clean and beautified Earth; and She shall be joyful for Her release from bondage and renewal, for long hast She been in bondage and crying for release. I say. The new residents shall be as ones which have been prepared to partake of her joy and release, for there shall go forth a great cry of joy, and it shall manifest as a Great and Shining Light about the Earth.

And it shall be seen from afar; and man shall navigate the seas by the light which is made manifest therefrom. I say unto thee: A great and shining star shall be the Point of such heavenly Light; and it shall shed its radiance about and above all the residences of the new earth. And they shall walk and weary not, for they shall be one with the radiance.

I tell thee of a surety: Thou shall see and be one with it. And so great shall be thy joy - so great shall be thy JOY, thou shall sing out: "Praise The Father Solen Aum Solen. Praise Him All Ye Host, Praise Him!! Joy! Joy! shall fill the Earth! So let it be - for this have I spoken.

* * * * * * * * * * * *

Be ye as the Hand of Me made manifest and give unto them this My Word, and I tell thee: There is little time that they have, for it is now come when there shall be a part given unto them which shall be as nothing known unto them, for they shall be as ones scattered and sorely oppressed - I say, sorely oppressed.

Let no man blame another for his plight, for I say unto them: They shall not stand blameless for their plight. I say, they are not blameless, for they have not reckoned with the Law. I say, they shall come to know the Truth of Mine Words; so, let it suffice them that which I have said.

I say: Prepare thineself for the Greater Part. Put aside thine hatred, bigotry, thine puny ways, thine hypocrisy, and all thine conceit. Let it be for thine own sake; I say: Put it away from thee, and ye shall prosper by thine obedience unto the Law!

I have spoken unto them which have ears; they shall harken unto Mine Words and remember them.

I AM Sananda

* * * * * * * * * * *

Be ye as the Hand of Me made manifest and give unto them this Mine Word. Let it be known that I Am Come; I walk within their midst as Man. I walk and talk as Man, yet they know Me not. I say unto them: Behold Me, I Am Como - I AM COME. I shall do that which I come for to do, then I shall withdraw even as I come, and I shall go unto Mine Father which hast sent Me.

Now, I say unto them: "Behold in Me the Light; See ye the Light, Know ye the light, walk ye in it, and be ye one with it." For I say unto thee: I AM the Light which lighteth every man's way. I Am He - I Am HE! - I AM HE!! I say unto them: I Am He which is come that they be unbound. Yet I tell thee: Ye shall follow where I lead thee, for I know the Way. And for this do I say: "Follow ye Me, for I know the way unto Mine Father's House."

Let it be known that I have called unto them, and unto them which answer the call I shall reveal many new things, and I shall shew unto them greater things than they have dreamed of. So be it that they shall prove themself before Me, and I shall prove Mine Sayings, for I speak not idly. I Am He Which hast kept Mine Covenant with Mine People, and I say, it is now come when I shall gather unto Mineself Mine Own, and they shall be prepared for the Greater Part. Hold out thine hand and I shall lead thee into paths of Righteousness. So be it as spoken.

* * * * * * * * * * *

Be ye as the Hand of Me made manifest and record that which I say unto thee. Let it be known that which I say, and I shall be as one responsible for Mine Own Words. I say, I am responsible for Mine Words, and woe unto anyone whosoever which puts words into Mine Mouth. Woe unto the ones which deny Mine Words, and unto him which tries to put his hand unto Mine Mouth.

I say unto him: "Behold The Lord God Which I Am." I Am Come that ye be lifted up; and the Word of God is Holy, without blemish - Pure. I say, let it remain so, and it shall serve thee well. Yet I say: "Hold thine tongue." Put no words into Mine Mouth, for I shall spew them out. Yet I say: Ye shall not set foot against Mine Prophet, for I have raised up prophets amongst the idolaters and the whoremongers, the infidels and the hypocrites.

I say, I have raised up Prophets; the Emissaries I have sent amongst the bigots and hypocrites, and they have persecuted them. They have blasphemed The Word; they have turned out Mine Servants and gone from them. I say, they shall hear that which I say, for I shall deal justly with them. I shall cause them to stand still and listen. For I come not that the Law be set aside; I come that it be made known. So let it be, for it shall profit them to know.

I say, they which have blasphemed against The Word and set foot against Mine Servants shall come to account for their words, their deeds. Let it be known: Their names stain the pages of the Book of Life, for they have written therein their own name splashed with blood; upon their hands they have the stain of blood, for they are the ones responsible for the martyrdom of many a Saint - many a Prophet. Now they ask, "Why this thing be visited upon me? Have I not prayed unto God for deliverance?" I say, behold thine garments, dyed with blood of Mine Servants. I say: Stand ye aside, let them pass, let them pass, I say. For they wear the spotless linen.

It is they which wear the Crown of Victory! I say unto the bigots and the hypocrites: Stand ye aside and let them pass, for they have served Me. Now they shall pass thru the Portal of Mine Abode, and they shall find therein surcease from their persecution, from their labors amongst the idolaters and blasphemers. I declare unto thee this day: I Am Come that they be delivered out. So shall it be.

* * * * * * * * * * *

Be ye as ones which have been given the Word; and as ye are given, ye are Guardians of The Word and ye shall be responsible for that which ye do with it. It is said, ye shall take nothing away, add nothing unto, and it shall be regarded as Sacred. Ye shall place upon it no puny interpretation of thine own, for ye shall be as one illumined, when thou hast so purified thineself as to receive of Me. Mine Seal and Mine Authority I shall give unto thee and ye shall stand spotless before Me, for I say unto thee: Come before Me blameless and as one of clean hands. Confess not thine sins before man, and attempt to conceal them from Me. I say unto thee, O man, I Am the Knower and I Am the Doer. I Am the giver and the taker. I am not a puny god. I Am The One Sent that there be Light - so let it be. As The Father hast willed it, so shall it be.

Behold The Light which I AM

* * * * * * * * * * * *

Be ye as the Hand of Me made manifest unto them and give unto them this Word, and it shall profit them to receive that which I have for them, for it is now come when there shall be Great Revelations. And Great Wonders shall be made known unto them which now stand with their hands before their face, seeing not.

I say: Great and Glorious are the Works of The Father; Great and Glorious are the marvels yet to be revealed unto man; for 1 say he knows not the fullness of The Father's House; he knows not the worlds yet to be revealed unto him. I say that the Heavens shall give up their Secrets, and man shall know the fullness thereof. Yet it is said, as he is prepared, so shall he receive. So be it and Selah.

Wherein is it said that great is the inheritance of man, for is he not the Son of God - is he not created in the image of God? According unto the image which Our Father held, so did He create man. Yet he, man, hast wandered afar from his perfection. He hast become lost; he knows not from whence he came, neither whence he goeth. He hast lost his way. Yet I say, he shall find his way, for the trail is clearly, plainly marked, and it is strait and narrow.

Now I say, many come that he be brot back into his place of abode wherein he shall know himself as he is. It is the way of flesh to cry out, and it is given unto mortal man to be as the wayward son, crying out in his misery and darkness, knowing not which way to go, not which way to turn. Yet I say, look up, man of Earth: Look up; Behold the Glory of the Heavens. See that which God hast done. I say, behold ye the Heavens and know ye the fullness thereof, for it is now come when ye shall pass beyond the barrier of flesh.

I say, Pass, let it be known that there are greater Glories than man hast seen with mortal eyes. I say, behold ye the glory of heaven. It is said, "In Mine Father's House are many mansions, and I say unto thee, these Mansions are inhabited. Yea, are they inhabited with Beings, and many not unlike thine own self - many unlike thineself.

It is said: Man goes from Glory unto Glory; yea, Greater and Greater Glory shall he know, for the fullness of his Glory he hast not glimpsed as yet. Now it is come when his concept of himself shall be as the foolishness of babes, for he shall arise as on wings and he shall dwell in heights yet undreamed. I say: Man is destined for the Stars, and the Earth shall be his footstool.

So be it and Selah

* * * * * * * * * * *

Be ye as Mine Hand made manifest unto them and record for them this Mine Word, and it shall profit them to receive it. Let it be given unto them as I give it unto thee, and it shall suffice them that I Am The One

Sent that they be lifted up. For this I come, and for this am I here. I Am The Lord of Lords, The Host of Hosts, and I say unto thee this day: It is now come when Great and Glorious work shall be accomplished, and Great shall be the Glory of the new day.

I say, great shall be the glory of the New Day, for it shall bring forth Great Light and marvels such as man hast note known. And man shall no longer be bound unto the Earth, neither shall he be bound by the attraction of the moon, for it shall hold no attraction for him. He shall break his own bounds, and he shall arise as the Phoenix, and swift shall be his ascent; I say, swift shall be his ascent.

And he shall be swift as the arrow in its flight, and sure his mark. For say, he shall know whither he goest, and it shall profit him. Let it be known that the doors shall swing wide before him; yet he shall be as one prepared to enter in. It shall be for the good of all that he pass within the boundaries of the Heavens yet unexplored.

Now I say, it is come when the doors stand ajar, and man of Earth shall pass when he hast so prepared himself. Yet there is a time and a way, and it shall come to pass that he shall be as the porter - he shall find his way, and none shall so say him nay.

For when he hast so prepared himself, he prepared himself he shall arise as on wings, and he shall make his ascent as the Mighty Falcon; he shall be independent of all gadgets - all clumsy machinery.

He shall go out as one swift in flight, unafraid and with dignity; I say, with dignity he shall go out unafraid, and as one prepared. Let it be.For the time is now come when men of Earth shall come to know that which hast been mysterious unto them. Now it is come when the Book of Life shall be read and understood.

So let it be, for this have I spoken

* * * * * * * * * * *

Be ye as the hand of Me and give unto them this Mine Word, and it shall profit them to receive it in the Name of Mine Father which hast sent Me.

I now say unto them which have ears to hear, be ye alert that no man trip thee up, that no man be unto thee a stumbling block, that no man give unto thee the bitter cup. Let it be known that there are traitors amongst thee, that there are false gods, false doctrines. And false gods there shall be, false doctrines there shall be, traitors there shall be - yet I say unto thee, follow them not. Be ye as one wise unto their schemes - their wiles and cunning ways.

I say unto thee, Watch, Look, See, know them for that which they are. See their works and be ye as one prepared for to go the last mile with Me, for I shall show thee many things which are new and strange unto thee. Give ye not the bitter cup unto Mine Servants, for I say unto thee, there are ones which stand by prepared to go the last mile with them, and they shall be delivered out from the Earth as ones free from the gravity of the Earth and the attraction of the Moon. I say, they shall be freed forever. So be it. I know - I KNOW, I KNOW whereof I speak; so let it suffice that I Am The Lord thy God. Be it so. So be it.

I AM Sananda

* * * * * * * * * * *

Sori Sori: Be ye as the hand of Me and give unto them this Mine Word, and it shall suffice them. They shall bear witness of Mine Word and they shall hold it Sacred; and they shall be as ones blest to be a part of the Plan which now unfolds before them. I say they shall be blest. So let it be, for this do I give unto them this Mine Word: Whatever be done in the world of man is with the intent of man, for man hast been given the Law - the mind with which to work.

It is now come when the world of man is in a precarious state, and he hast not the mind to be his own deliverer his own Savior, for he hast gone far afield. He hast entangled himself and now he finds himself entangled in all manner of conditions which are foreign unto him. He hast not the strength, neither the wisdom to untangle his affairs; therefore, it behooves Me to send into his midst one which shall have the Wisdom and Power; for He is trained well in the affairs of governments; and these things bother Him not neither shall they confuse Him.

So be it that He shall walk with the heads of government, and He shall counsel them and lead them in the way in which they shall go, while many shall turn Him away, heeding not His counsel. These shall be as the fools, for I say unto the man of Earth: He shall take heed of Mine Word, and he shall be as one prepared to enter into the Great and Mighty Council which is The Over-All Council.

Now it is for this that the Earth hast been exiled - that She hast been in quarantine, for She hast been a wayward planet, giving footing to many generations of rebels - "Rebels," I say. These rebels have rebelled against the Law - The Word of God, and they have been as the Prodigal Son. I say, they have rebelled against the High and Mighty Council, for they have not accepted that which hast been set before them. They speak of peace. Peace? Wherein is peace to be found in them? I say, let peace be established within thine heart, and no man shall take it from thee. Bear ye in mind, I Am Come that it be established amongst men - that it be established within the heart of men. Peace? Wherein is it written that peace shall reign within thine heart? I say, be ye as one at peace, and ye shall be as one with Me.

Let it be said this day: I am not alone. I bring with Me a mighty host - a number of warriors - well trained in the affairs of governments; they are well qualified to meet all the situations which confront men of Earth.

Now I say again that one shall be sent into all the chambers wherein sit the High and Mighty Counselors of the Law, and He shall do a mighty work. Yet the time is not yet come when each and every one shall pay heed unto His counsel. Be ye ever mindful of these Mine Words, and let not thine foot slip. Pay ye heed unto that which I have said; feign not wisdom for thou art amongst the unknowing which hast been enmeshed within the tangled web which now threatens to engulf thy civilization and destroy it completely - forever. So I say unto thee, be ye as one patient and love thine neighbor as thyself; call no man a fool until thou hast proven thine own wisdom. Wash thine own hands before thou callest his dirty. Bless thyself by the cleansing. Be ye as one thotful of Mine Word, Mine Work, Mine Counsel, and I shall take thot of thee. So be it I have: spoken and pray thou hearest Me.

* * * * * * * * * * *

Sori Sori: Be ye as one on whose shoulders I place Mine Mantle, and I say unto thee, I Am The Lord God, Sent of Mine Father that all men be lifted up. Therefore, I say unto them, lift up thine feet and come; come out from amongst the people which hast portioned out the poison for themself. Hear ye Me, and bring thyself out from amongst them which violate the Law. I say, ye shall dare be different, and ye shall walk in the way I lead thee.

Ye shall fear not the scorn of man, neither shall ye fear the wrath of men, their weapons, nor the pity of their plight. And the words of their mouth shall fall upon thine ears as a breeze blown by a gentle wind; ye shall not heed that which they say; ye shall follow after Me, The Lord Thy God, and I shall lead thee out of the pit, and ye shall not fail. No man shall drag thee down, for I shall sustain thee in all thine ways. Ye shall know the truth, and it shall set thee free. So be it and Selah.

Mine Word is sacred and Holy, and no man shall invalidate it. No man shall set his hand unto Mine Mouth, for I shall say that which is needful and expedient. I shall put Mine foot against the Door wherein the profane would rush in. I shall put asunder the works of the wicked, and it shall be as ash beneath the feet of the righteous, for I shall not surrender up Mine People.

I shall not fail thee in thine trial and in thine time of want, for I am a just and righteous man, which hast gone before thee, and I know whereof I speak, and I am prepared to go all the way with thee. Bear ye witness of Me, walk with Me and know ye that I Am with thee. Be ye not deceived by their garments and pretty speeches. For I say, they come in a variety of costumes claiming to be "He," and they know not that they blaspheme the Name of the One in whose Name I Come. I say, they know not the name of Solen Aum Solen. They know not that which they do, for they are want to storm the Gate. Yet I say, I Am the Porter at the gate and I know them. Let them first learn the way of

Righteousness, and they shall walk in the Way I set before them, and they shall walk gently and be at peace - they shall Know peace.

Be it so, and so be it. For this do I speak unto thee – that they might know that which I say. Let it be well with thee, for I Am with thee unto the end.

* * * * * * * * * * *

Say unto them: The Word of God shall be as a Two-Edged Sword. It shall cut away all that which hast bound them and that which hast held them in bondage lo these eons, and it shall bring to light that which hast been hidden. While I say it shall cut away all that hast bound them, it shall free them and they shall be aware of their freedom.

Wherein is it said that one shall walk amongst them which is prepared to bear witness of Me, and one which shall be qualified to set in order the affairs of the Nations. I say, one shall come into thy midst which shall be as one prepared to set in order the affairs of State, and He shall bear witness of Me, for He shall know the Law and be as One qualified to give unto the people counsel.

And they shall raise up and follow Him knowingly and willingly, for He shall be as the one which is sent that they be lifted up. They shall hear His name for the first time in High places as the one long expected, and they shall be sorely oppressed at the time of His pronouncements. For He shall be as One which hast come at the appointed hour, when the hearts of men are sorely tried, heavy and sore. Tearful shall be the women of all the lands and fearful shall be the youths of all the lands, for they shall be confused and weary.

While I say the old men shall shake their heads and deny Him in their fearfulness and in their ignorance, they shall shout their slanderous sayings which they are so wont to use against the fortune of men (their benefactors). Now it is come when they shall begin to bestir themself, for they have long awaited this day.

Yet they shall not see the finish of the Work this One shall do, for His reign shall be long and good. And no man shall turn Him aside or overthrow Him, for He shall come in Power and with great Strength, for He shall bear the Crown of Royalty. He shall be as One on whose head rests the Crown of the House of Israel, for He Hast been as One prepared for long. Long hast He awaited this day when He might take up His reign. So be it a triumphant reign, and mighty shall be His Work. I say, behold ye the One which is to come, for He shall wear the Crown of Victory.

For this does He come

* * * * * * * * * * *

Sori Şori: Be ye as one prepared to do that which I give unto thee to do, for it shall be for the good of all mankind, and it shall be for their sake that I shall send, one unto them which shall bear witness of Me, the Lord thy God. Bear ye in mind that I Am The One Which hast held the Earth and the children thereof in the palm of Mine Hand, and I am not of a mind to let Her go down into destruction. Therefore, I shall do that which I will, and I am one on whose shoulders rests great responsibility, for I shall choose the method by which I shall perform My Work, and I shall perform a mighty service unto all mankind. Therefore, I shall do a strange thing that they be healed of their blindness and deafness; they shall see, and know that they see. Therefore, I say unto them, Come and See - Come and Hear - Come and Know and be healed. Say unto them in Mine Name that He Is Come that all men be lifted up, and it is so. Fortune thineself the Greater Part; Bless thineself and I shall do Mine Part, for I Am The Way, The Truth and The Light.

* * * * * * * * * * *

Be ye as the Hand of Me made manifest and give unto them this Word, and let it suffice them that it is Mine - not thine - surely not theirs, for they which set foot against thee, set foot against Me, The Lord God. For I AM The Lord God, The King of Kings, The Host of Hosts - and I say, them which set foot against thee set foot against Me. I Am He which hast called thee out from amongst them, and I have led thee into this place; I have given unto thee a part - a place - and a King's ransom I have saved for thee. So be it I shall do that which I have declared I shall do, for I am not a deceiver. I Am He which is Sent that they be delivered out of bondage. So let them seek the Light and accept Mine Servants which I have prepared. So be it, I have prepared thee with Mine Own Hand - so let it suffice thee.

* * * * * * * * * * *

Recorded by Sister Thedra - of the order of the Emerald Cross, the Brotherhood of the Seven Rays.

Recorded by Sister Thedra

THE PART OF COUNSEL

1

By the hand of One Sent shall ye receive the first part of a New Work, and it shall begin this day - so let it be. It shall be brot forth as the other which hast been done. Ye shall bring forth this work as nothing before, and it shall be for the good of all that it is done -- so let it be. Ye shall set aside a place wherein ye shall do the work, and wherein none shall distract thee; and ye shall be as one prepared - so be it and Selah. Ye shall arise at an hour suitable and put thine house in order, and come into the place which hast been set aside, and it shall be given unto thee. So let it begin now, and it shall begin with this part herein, and it shall be the first of the New Part.

2

Say unto them in this manner: That the law shall be the law; yet the law of one realm holds good for that realm only -- and likewise is the law changed from time to time -- each people, each age. And this is to be understood: That one law holds good for one people in one realm; yet others of other realms do not come under that law.

While there are laws which hold good thruout ALL the inhabited Universes, created and peopled, yet concern not thyself with these now, for at this time thou needst but be concerned with thine own place and part -- thine own orb and part which ye play at this present time. I say, this is the day to be concerned with -- this place, plan, and work at hand.

And it shall profit thee little to ask what the Earth rests on while thine feet are sinking in quicksand.

I say: Let it be understood that there are Ones which have come from lands afar, which have been prepared to assist thee in this place wherein thou art within the Earth - the world of man - and the foolishness of man is as naught unto them. They hear not the foolish prayers of the selfish man, neither the cries of the unjust for they, too, come under a law, by which they are allowed to enter into the world of man.

They come as ones prepared, and by the consent of the Mighty Council. They bring with them naught; they come empty-handed, and they ask naught. They give of themselves, and for this their reward shall be great, for theirs is a Selfless Mission. Now I say unto thee: Be ye as one prepared to receive of these which come to assist thee. They walk amongst thee as ones unsung, unknown, and they ask only that ye be prepared to hear them out, and that ye be prepared for the Greater Part. So be it, as ye are prepared so shall ye receive.

* * * * *

3

Sori Sori: I say unto thee: Ye shall give unto them which seek wisdom this part, and it shall profit them to accept it, for I have chosen this time and method to give it unto them. This Mine Word shall be the Word of God as set forth in its purity - yet I say, thine language is insufficient to express the fullness of the perfection of The Word of God; neither can the beauty be captured by word or pen. Neither hast there lived a man upon the Earth which hast known the fullness of the grandeur of Heaven, for he hast not experienced it – and until he hast experienced it he knows not.

Now I say: It is come when there shall be ones which know shall visit thee, and they shall call thee by name and they shall tell thee of things which thou hast not seen, neither heard. They shall be unto thee great Light, and direct thee in this part. They shall bring unto thee great Knowledge and strength.

Now I say unto thee, O Reader: Be ye not mistaken about this, for I am the Author and Finisher of Mine Work. I have begun a Great Work and I shall finish it, and no man shall say Me Nay!

While ye sleep I shall do a Work ye now not of. Ye shall learn well thine lessons, then ye shall know wherein I have spoken, and ye shall remember well that which I have said.

Blest are they which learn of Me and by Me. So let thine mind be staid upon Me, The Light, for I AM THE LIGHT - out of the Light I come. I am not limited to time or space; l am One with The ALL, known as Solen Aum Solen, The Father.

I Am Sent that this day bear fruit and that the harvest be brot forth this day. So let it suffice that I am The One Sent that ye be awakened - so be it I come that it be accomplished this day.

While I speak unto thee in simple language that ye might comprehend, I say, too, that it is given in this manner for a reason which ye know not. Therefore, I beseech thee, criticize not the manner in which I give this Word, for it behooves thee to seek the meaning thereof, and hold thine tongue, for in thine criticism thou hast lost favor with Me - in thine deceit and bigotry thou hast not found favor with Me.

I say: Come unto me as a little child. Put away thine conceit and thine puny ways, and I shall put within thine mouth Mine Words. I shall touch thee and make of thee a prophet in thine own right.

I have given unto this, Mine Servant, the Authority and power to speak for Me, and I have lain Mine hand upon her head and pronounced the Word which hast prepared her to receive Me and of Me - and she hast accounted for herself in the time of stress. She hast remained true unto her trust, and she hast not betrayed herself or her trust. I now give unto her this dictation, and she shall prepare it for them which seeks after such as she hast prepared for them.

And according to Mine command she shall not trespass upon anyone, neither shall she put words into thy mouth. She shall do that which I ask of her, and she shall not trespass on thy free will. So be it I have sibored her for this day, and the days which are yet to come.

Behold ye the Work of The Lord. Behold ye the Hand of God; see it move, for it shall move the length and breadth of the Earth. It shall move before it all which shall oppose it, the Light. It shall bring into the Light all that is of the Light, and that which is not of the Light shall be no more seen of man, for it shall return unto its nothingness.

I AM COME that I might set men aright - set them upright upon their feet - that they might bear their own weight and be responsible for their own deeds and for themself. Each shall study well himself - his deeds and the responsibility thereof.

I come that he be made responsible. So be it that I AM HE which is Sent at this time for this part, and I shall not stop Mine Work until I am finished!

Think ye, O man, that I am a puny priest, one of failure and exile? Neither have I forgotten Mine Part, Mine Office, for I have been ordained of Mine Father for this part which I shall finish with honor and dignity.

I shall triumph over evil and put to shame the evil doer, the slanderer and the whoremonger, the hypocrites and blasphemers. For I shall do a wondrous Work, and they shall stand ashamed before Me, for they shall see themself as they are. I say unto thee, O man of Earth: Cleanse thineself of all deceit, hypocrisy and bigotry, and prepare thineself for the days ahead, for ye shall continue thine days after thou hast put aside thine mortal flesh.

Be ye not deceived in this - think not to escape the Law. Enter into no unholy alliance with the forces of darkness, for I tell thee of a surety, they would deceive thee. For it is the Law: "As ye are prepared so shall ye receive." Give unto this much thot; ponder well Mine Word, and be ye mindful of Mine Sayings, for it shall profit thee much.

Now I come as a thief in the night - I find thee off guard - thou hast been babbling and mumbling the sayings of the Ancients of times long past. Yet I ask of thee: Think ye were one of them? Think ye were there? Then why mumble? Then why turn unto these ancient words, when I place before thee the present day that which shall feed thee and satisfy thine longings and fill thine needs? I bring unto thee this day a part designed to fill thine needs and to prepare thee for the days ahead.

It is now come when man shall stand shorn of all self-glory, of all his pomp and ceremony, and he shall stand as naked before the Great and Mighty Tribunal. He shall be as one exposed unto the Light wherein all things are revealed.

So be it I say: Cleanse out all the impure thots, all the Impure - and beat not thine breast in supplication to any ancient priest or lord, for I say unto thee: Cleanse thine own temple, and I shall enter in and abide with thee. Put no name above The Name of Solen Aum Solen, The One Which hast given unto thee Being. Let no man say unto thee "there is One higher." Yet I say: HE, Solen Aum Solen IS; has always been; yet He hast been called many names in many tongues; and the Name matters not. For this day I speak unto thee of THIS DAY - and ye which speak the language in which I am speaking shall be set apart for a Work which shall be different from all other. Ye shall be designated by a number and a color, and ye shall stand - stand upon the Precepts of The Mighty and Holy Council which hast brot forth a Mighty Country.

I say, ye shall stand upon the Precepts and Concepts which hast been set forth in the founding of thy Mighty Nation. Ye shall stand as a people apart from all others.

Yet ye shall not adorn thyself in fine raiment and boast of thine success while thy brothers crawl on their bellies before thee begging bread.

I say, ye shall stand apart as a living example of the Light which I AM. Ye shall not be as the idolaters; ye shall worship only the Source of thy being; and ye shall not give unto any man the power to forgive thee thine transgressions - neither shall any man give unto thee passport into the Heavenly Kingdoms.

It is said: "Ye shall have no false gods - NO GOD - before Me." So be it that I say unto thee: Have none save The Father of ALL -- The O - Solen Aum Solen, for thou art ensouled in Him - in Him thou hast thine BEing, and there is naught save Him.

Bring unto Him thineself in Holy Reverence and ask of Him forgiveness, and cleanse out the unseen places wherein thou hast hidden thine inmost thots and deeds. Know ye, nothing is hidden from Him, for HE is THE ALL-SEEING EYE.

Be ye as a little child; hold out thy hand in humble submission unto His Will, and He shall give unto thee according unto thy preparation.

* * * * *

4

Sori Sori: Let this be unto them Mine Testimony, that they might know from whence cometh the Authority for this part and for this Word. I say unto thee, I have given unto thee power and the authority to speak in Mine Name, and thou hast not put thine hand into their pockets, neither have they troubled themself to assist thee. Yet I say, I shall bring forth one which shall give unto thee assistance which is needful, and he shall find his reward great, for I say there is such unknown wealth stored up for him as he hast not seen. Yet he shall ask no reward on Earth nor in Heaven, for he shall serve for the joy of serving - so be it that he shall ask no other reward.

Now ye shall bring forth a New Part, and this one shall be called "The Part of Counsel" - the part which is for the Counselors. The

Council shall direct and put forth such Work as is needful at this time, and when there is a need it shall be filled - this I declare unto thee.

Before there is another moon, ye shall see many changes, and many new things shall be shown unto thee. While it is not yet time to reveal all which shall be shown unto thee, ye shall wait for the time and place. I have said I shall bring thee into a place and show thee many new things, and it is so. So be it ye shall abide with Me and wait upon Mo, and I shall deal justly with thee.

* * * * *

5

While I say I shall deal justly with thee, I say: As ye give so shall ye receive. So be it that I give unto thee of Mineself - so shall it be with thee - and they which receive of thee shall be unto thee mindful of Me, for as I have given unto thee and thou hast given unto them, so do they receive of Me - thru thee. Therefore, it is required of them to be mindful of thee, for art thou not Mine Servant? And is a Servant not the representation of his Master's House? And is he not worthy of recognition? So be it that I send thee forth as Mine Messenger - as Mine hand and foot made manifest unto them.

I have Ordained thee Mine Priestess, and Mine Priestess shall be honored for the Service rendered unto mankind in Mine Name. So be it I have spoken and thou hast heard Me, and thou hast recorded it as I have spoken. So be it this shall be made available unto them which hunger for Light, for I say unto them: I have set One apart and Ordained that One as Mine Priestess, and it behooves thee to know and to heed that which I say unto thee thru and by this means - and by her hand shall the Word of God go forth as it is spoken, without embellishment or change of any kind - for by this method shall I know the true from the false, for I have said unto thee: "Change not the WORD OF GOD," for it shall stand on its own merits.

I am now prepared to speak of thine own world - of preparation and many things concerning thee and that which ye know not of.

Let it be said that there are ones now within thine midst which are prepared to give unto thee the Cup of Living Water, and they shall be as Mine hands and as Mine feet. They shall be fleet of foot and quick of Spirit, for Mine Spirit shall abide in them, and they shall know themself to be One with Me.

They shall commune with Me, and they shall not be deceived, for they shall know Me for that which I AM, The Lord of Lords, The Host of Hosts, and I AM HE which is Sent that a Mighty Work be done - so shall it be according to The Father's Will.

* * * * *

6

Before We proceed with this Work, let it be understood that there are ones which deny Me, Mine existence, Mine Word, Mine Servants. Yet I say, they but betray themself. They are want to know me, and they but deny The Father which hast Sent Me - for as they deny Me, so do they deny The Father Solen Aum Solen, THE SOURCE OF THEIR BEING. And as they deny Mine Servant, Mine Word - so do they deny Me.

I Am Come that they might KNOW! Yet they fear – they fear for themself, for their fortunes, for their children! Yet when I reach out Mine hand unto them that they be lifted up, I hear them say: It is an impossible situation; it is an incurable disease; it is an absolute thing which no man can correct, no man can change - and they call Me an imposter!

Poor, impoverished are they, for they have been under the yoke for long, and they are yet bound unto the old order - might I say the old "order of thinkers"? Yea, they think themselves to be thus and so while they go about as robots. They think not in their own right; they have no thots of their own, for all inspiration comes from Spirit, whether it be for weal or woe. None are without guidance, be it high or low - I say, "None are without guidance!!" While I say: "Each unto his own preparation shall he receive" (for it is the Law).

Now I speak unto them which are prepared to receive this Mine Word - and none shall deny it.

There is a place prepared for each and every Being which exists, even in all worlds. There is a time allotted unto each and every one. There is a plan which is given unto each one as he comes into physicality, and he knows the part which he is to play. Yet there are many - too many - which forget. These I am speaking to now.

I say: Arise ye which sleepeth! Arise ye which are dead! Arise ye which hear Mine Voice, and I shall touch thee; I shall quicken thee and ye shall KNOW even as I KNOW.

I say: Follow ye Me, for I have gone before thee - I know the way. It is for this that I bid thee follow Me, for I have gone the long way to find thee. I have called unto thee thru the centuries; I have searched thee out; I have stood thee upright on thine feet, and thou hast fallen asleep again - yea - even on thine feet thou hast thou slept! Thou hast fallen asleep even in Mine embrace.

Now I say, thou hast slept overtime. Now ye shall awaken and come forth as ones alive - as ones willing to stay awake.

Think ye not that I shall always abide with thee, for I shall take Mine leave of thee - even as I come. Is it not said that "I shall come as a thief in the night"? Wast it not done - wast it not so? I came! Didst thou know the day - the hour? I say unto thee, thou knew not the hour? Neither shall ye know the hour of Mine departure.

Now, fain would I speak unto thee of thine frailties - thine weakness - for thou knowest them; thou seest them. Yet ye shall not point thine finger at thine fellow men, for are they worse or better than thou? Wherein hast thou attained perfection? Call not thine brother foolish so long as thou thinkest thine ownself to be wise, for I say: Ye know not the freedom of the Universe; ye know not the freedom of man. Thou art bound, even in thine thinking! I say, ye know not how nor what to think, for thou art a confused people - a confused people, I say!!

I come that ye might KNOW, that ye might learn of Me the Law of the Universe - the Law which makes all men One.

I am the Law-giver for this day. I come not to set aside the old laws - yet to reveal unto thee greater Law. For it is now come when man shall expand his world, and he shall pass beyond his boundaries, as ones free from the gravitation of the Earth and the attraction of the moon.

So be it I am well prepared for Mine Part, for long have I been traversing the Universe - yea, the Universes without number do I know; as the palm of Mine hand I know them. So be it I say unto thee: Arise! and come unto Me, and I shall show unto thee greater glories than thou hast dreamed of. So be it I am He which guards the Portal, and I shall guard well the Portal, for all within is Mine. All that is without is as nothing to me. I say: All that is within is Mine, for I am the Keeper of Mine Father's Fortune. All that He has He hast endowed unto Me - I shall not betray Mine trust.

I speak unto thee of the Universes without number - I <u>Know</u> the number thereof. Knowest thou the number of the stars in the heavens?

I say unto thee: Thou knowest not the Stars in thy heavens. Yet there are more Universes than stars visible unto thine sight.

I say unto thee: BEHOLD THE GLORY OF THE HEAVENS! And be ye as one blest. Behold the handiwork of thy God Which created the Earth and the Heavens thereof!!

* * * *

7

Sori Sori: Mine hand I place upon thine head, and I speak the Word which shall be unto thee the Authority to speak in Mine Name and to use Mine Name - and for the good of ALL mankind shall it be.

Now ye shall place thine hand in Mine and I shall direct thee into the place wherein ye shall be given yet greater power. And by the Grace of Mine Father shall it be done unto thee, even as it is done unto Me.

So be it that there stands by a Mighty Host to assist in the Work at hand, and it shall be done. No man shall say unto US, nay, for We shall stand as Sentinels over them which have volunteered to serve Life in the physical flesh. I say, they serve not alone, for flesh is weak indeed, and it is for Us of the Host that they receive their strength and direction. I say, it is from the Host which stands by that they receive their strength and direction. We direct their activities and give unto them strength to carry out their activity which they have chosen - even before taking embodiment in flesh.

While I say there are ones which stand by as Sentinels, I too say that They neither force nor coerce; They neither persuade nor hinder; They wait for the one who would serve, to offer up himself in Holy surrender as the living sacrifice, that all mankind might be blest.

There are ones who say, "Help me!" Yet wherein have they given that they be helped? Wherein have they helped? I say: It is within every man's capacity to do something to lift up his fellow-man - yet he does nothing that lifts him, while he puts his hand into the pocket of another and asks alms from them. There are ones which give of his earthly substance, while he does it grudgingly. He finds no reward in this, for it shall return unto him as a burning and flaming sword.

There are ones which administer unto the sick grudgingly, yet they find they are not comforted, neither shall they find comfort - for they have not given of themself. Therefore the gift is not considered valid - for without the giver, the gift is invalid in the sight of The Father.

So be it there are ones which give for the self-gratification, to be seen of men, to receive of them praise and esteem. These have already received their reward, for none other shall they find - none other!

There are ones which give of themself, and this is the gift which is acceptable unto The Lord of Lords, The King of Kings, The Father Solen Aum Solen. So be it the only gift which HE can accept - therein is the Secret of man's greatest joy.

Blest is the giver when the gift is bestowed with love and joy, and with the joy which is of the heart.

Blest is the one which gives of his substance - yet greater is the Gift of <u>Selfless Service</u>, for this is the accredited gift in Our sight.

Blest is he which receives such gifts given in selfless service, for they are the recipients of Love. That is the Love of which I speak - the Selfless Love. Yet there are ones which know not the meaning of Love. Unto these I say: Go into the stables and watch the mother with her lamb; the mother with her foal; the mother with her calf; and see if thine love is any greater, any higher, any <u>greater</u>, I say.

When thou canst love with the greater Love, thou hast risen out of the stable!

I say unto thee: Arise, and be ye as a fit vessel to serve Me in Mine place of abode.

Be ye as one brot forth this day on the wings of Love. Be ye as one acceptable unto The Lord of Hosts, and be ye as one called out, and ye shall be given a place upon the right hand of God The Father, and HE shall bless thee and ye shall be glad.

Many are called - few are chosen - Why? They have not kept their covenant - they have betrayed themself. These shall sorrow mightily, for they shall be cast aside to wait in darkness. They shall know not the joy of the one which sits upon The Father's right hand.

There are ones which go forth preaching strange and false doctrines - these are as the fools, prattling the sayings of the ancients or moderns. These are as the ones which are led about by some unknown, untried Spirit which makes mockery of the "Spirit." And they are in no wise learned of the LAW - the GREATER LAW - the LAW under which they live and have their being.

They are to be pitied, for they know not that they do not know - they <u>think</u> themself wise. Yet I say, poor in Spirit are they, for they are as ones under a "spell." They are deluded from the first.

Wherein is it said that "There are ones which would lead thee astray and hold thee captive"? It is so; yet it is said: "I come that ye be led out of captivity; I come that ye be delivered out of bondage."

Therefore, it behooves thee to seek the Light, and I shall hear thine supplications and consider them. Let it be said that I am mindful of all thine goings, thine comings, and all thine deeds. Every thot I know, and I have said: Purify: thineself; put aside thine foolishness; ask of The Father forgiveness for all thine shortcomings; and One shall come unto thee and give unto thee as thou art prepared to receive - so shall it be.

* * * * *

8

Let it be known that there are ones which have betrayed themself many times. They have given of themself that the evil one be served. They have forgotten that which hast been given unto them to do - that which they came to do.

These are the ones which are now groping in darkness. They have the will to serve the Light, yet they know not which way to go. They cry out for help, knowing not from whence it cometh - and fearing their prayers are not heard. Yet unto them is given a part - the part of preparation.

They again are entrusted with the WORD, and they have but to accept it. While they have a fear of being deceived - they fear! They fear! And they turn unto their friends asking solace. Wherein have they been comforted? Now I ask, wherein have they found solace or comfort?

Blest is he which takes comfort of Me, for I shall touch luim, and he shall come to know Mine touch.

I come that these be awakened, that they might be brot out of their bondage, that they might come to know as I know.

Wherefore I bring with Me a Host of Helpers from the realm of Light - a band of Angelic helpers which have for a great part clothed themself in mortal flesh that this day might be the fulfilling of a great and mighty plan.

Therefore, I am come not alone. While thou hast slept a great Work hast been done - yet it is not finished - and thou hast not seen the finish thereof. It shall come to pass that man of this present generation shall arise as on the beams of Light, and he shall soar unto heights yet unknown unto him. Yet I say unto thee, O man: Be ye the unknowing one; be ye not puffed up in thy conceit, thine unknowing, for there are greater things in store for thee. Ye shall see yet greater things, for the heavens shall open up unto the just, and the wonders thereof shall be revealed unto them.

Be it so, and so be it that there are worlds unknown unto thee, O man. In thine darkness thou hast wondered and wandered; thou hast thot thineself isolated in a Universe so great that thou couldst not comprehend it.

Yea, in part it is so, for thou hast indeed been isolated - even in quarantine - for thou hast been as ones put aside as an "unclean" lot.

Now it is come when ye shall purify thineself, justify thineself, and ye shall stand before the Mighty Council as ones purified. Then ye shall pass thru the barrier, for then ye shall be as ones given passport into the Greater Realms.

Thou hast been clothed and fed thru the wisdom and mercy of the Great Council of which ye know but little. Yet thou hast boasted of thine wisdom and accomplishments. Thou hast accomplished naught alone, for as thou didst come into the world naked and helpless, thou wast provided. So be it that thou hast not seen the hand that hast made the provision for thee. Thinkest thou that thou hast made the Sun to bring forth the light - the moon to shine by night - the clouds to bring forth the rain?

O man: In thine unknowing thou hast fallen from Grace; in thine conceit thou hast become puffed up; thou hast boasted of thine accomplishments.

I ask of thee: From whence cometh thine inspiration? From whence cometh the Light, the strength, the mind, the wisdom?

Let it be known that the Earth - the heavens round and about - are Mine and the fullness thereof. I have prepared for thee long, long ere thou came into mortal flesh, that ye be provided; yea, I have a plan whereby ye shall be delivered out of thine perils.

I declare unto thee: I am the Provider, the Provender, and I AM HE which holds the plan within Mine hand. Yet man is given free will – he shall choose his way. While it is said: Thou hast chosen the hard way, it is now come when ye shall have a choice. Again ye shall make a choice, and I might say: I pray thee, may it be the one which shall profit thee - so may it ever be. So let it be - for this am I come.

* * * * *

9

By the Grace and Mercy of Mine Father, I come that ye be brot out of bondage. Now it is given unto Me to come as a thief in the night, and I find thee as ones unaware – unaware of thine plight, for thou art as ones in danger - in <u>danger</u>, I say! Yet thou hast fiddled and danced while the danger grows more apparent.

It is now time that ye alert thineself unto the danger which befronts thee. Too, I say, ye shall avail thineself of the assistance which We of the Mighty Council extend unto thee in this thine hour of need.

There are Ones which stand by to give assistance. Wherein is it said that thou art not sufficient unto thyself? Thou art <u>not</u> sufficient unto thineself, for thou hast not known thy peril; thou hast not seen thine need. So be it that ye know not that which shall be done to bring the

Earth and her heavens into their orb. The Earth hast long travailed, and it is for this that I come that this might be set aright.

As for man alone - he is never alone - he is NEVER alone. He hast ever been guarded, watched, and directed - yet he hast not been aware of his Guard, his Directors. His willfulness hast separated him from Them. He hast been as a cast-out, as an exile, a wayward son. While The Father calls unto him to return unto his abiding place, he gives, for the most part, little heed unto the call. For the most part he hast his fingers in his ears that he might not hear.

When it is come that he suffers greatly, he cries out for relief and strength. Yet when he is healed he goes his way in his forgetfulness, paying no heed unto them which hast been unto him succor.

There are ones which suffer for the sake of mankind. These are ones that have taken up the flesh garments that they do a work which shall profit their fellow men. These ask no reward save that they serve life in its full. I say, they ask naught of any man - they sacrifice self in selfless service. They are the ones which walk in silence and strut not before man - to be seen and heard of man - that they gain favor of him. They walk humbly and safely amongst the bigots and hypocrites, the infidels and the idol worshipers.

They fear no man - neither the tongue nor the foot do they fear. Yet it is said that the tongue of the asp stingeth not like the tongue of man. Too, it is said that: Woe unto anyone whichsoever that sets foot against one of Mine Servants. They fear not, for they know Mine hand is upon them. They ask not freedom from pain, that they escape the suffering; they ask not favors of Me The Lord God; they ask not for recognition of men. They are as ones which know wherein they are staid. They are satisfied to follow where I lead them. They fret not for small things. They are comforted that I am their Counselor - that I am with them and they know Mine Voice and respond unto it.

* * * * *

10

Sori Sori: There is a plan - a great and noble plan for man - and it behooves thee to know the part which thou hast chosen. I say unto thee, thou hast chosen a noble part.

Yet it is not an easy one, for the part thou hast chosen hast not been one of great favor with man - it is the part for which I have prepared thee. I have called thee forth as a Servant of The Great and Mighty God of Creation; I have ordained thee as the Son of God; I have given unto thee passport into Mine place of abode. And no man shall deny thee entrance: I say, PASS - pass ye shall. Place thine hand in Mine and I shall lead thee every step of the way - for this have I called thee forth. I know thee and thine every thot. I have watched thee, and I shall not forsake thee - neither shall Mine Word become invalid.

When it is come that man has made his final play within the flesh, he shall stand as one attired in yet another body - yet it shall be unlike the flesh. While he shall have the same pattern, he shall not have the atomic, heavy body of Earth's substance. He shall have a body which shall be of Light Substance - of the <u>Substance</u> of <u>Light</u>. He shall wear it as a garment, not unlike the one he hast worn, yet it shall not be unto him a bond - a bound. He shall have many bodies in his ascent, for he shall go from glory unto glory - each shall be more glorious, more beautiful, lighter. And at last he shall be free of all fetters, all bounds, ALL FETTERS, for AT LAST he shall be as I AM.

* * * * *

11

Sori Sori: I AM COME that man be lifted up – there is but little time allotted unto him, for his time within the Earth is but short. And at no time have I given unto him the Word which is designed to frighten him. Rather would I awaken him from his sleep.

He is asleep - some in deep sleep. Others have begun to stir, while others are awake. I say, for the most part man sleepeth yet.

Now it is come when certain ones shall go out from the Inner Temple which shall do a great and Mighty Work among men of Earth. They shall take up mortal flesh and walk among men as man. They shall come under the law of flesh. While others shall come as ones in flesh, which shall not come under the law of Earth, these shall appear as man. These shall do the work of man with the tools of man. Yet they shall supersede all man's achievements, for they shall have such knowledge that has as yet not been revealed unto man.

They shall be as the <u>revelators</u> - they shall bring with them such knowledge as man hast not yet dreamed. They shall prepare the way for yet others which are to follow them. For this do many wait that they come into the Earth, that they might be part of the New Earth, the establishing of "The New Earth." And they are well qualified, for they have been well schooled - they have been prepared in many a school which man of Earth hast not known.

It is said that many come from afar to study man and Earth that they might be prepared to assist in her preparation.

I say unto thee, O man of Earth: Thou art a curiosity unto others far afield. Thou art as ones groping in darkness. Thou as yet are not aware of thine own inheritance - yet ye boast in thine absolute ignorance. I say, thou art ignorant of the many schools wherein thine brothers labor that ye be helped, that ye be assisted at this time. Ye know not the number of Ambassadors and Messengers which have given of themself, that hast lowered their light to come into the Earth that man be enlightened.

Yet man in his ignorance hast profaned and defamed the Name of the One which hast been so merciful unto the wayward and unknowing ones as thou art.

I say, "Unknowing," for thou hast fallen from thine high estate. Thou hast fallen lower than the beast, for it is given unto the beast to be dumb - yet unto thee hast been given the gift of speech and thou hast adulterated it. Thou hast blasphemed the Word - the Name of thine Father which hast given unto thee BEing.

I say: Thou art slothful and affrighted, for thou hast "sinned" before HIM.

Thou hast fared far worse than the beast, for the beast knows no repentance. And it is given unto man to have the knowledge of right and wrong, for to know puts him in the class of man. Yet he repents not; he places himself in jeopardy, and his inheritance awaits him.

Or he repents and claims it - then he returns no more unto his filthy ways - unto his old ways. He goes forth as one sober and alert - as one aware of his Source - as one alive, and he gives credence unto his Source. He walks humbly, upright, as a Son of God. He bows before no false gods, he worships no idols, and he fortunes unto himself that which The Father Wills for him.

There is a time and a place set aside for each and every one, each unto his own preparation; each shall be in his own environment, as he hast prepared himself. There is no caste which shall hold him, yet he shall be as one which shall find himself in his place - and that shall be as he hast prepared for himself, for it is said: Prepare thyself for the Greater Part.

Yet I ask of thee: What hast thou done? What hast thou done? Hast thou repented? Hast thou turned thine face homeward? Hast thou loved thine neighbor as thine own self? Hast thou given of thineself that others be comforted? Hast thou given succor unto the comfortless - unto the sick and dying?

Or, hast thou sat in the seat of the bigot and appraised thine own worthiness greater than thine fellow man? Hast thou denied him comfort while thou hast wasted thy substance? Hast thou laughed at his foolishness while thou hast called thyself "wise"?

Now I ask of thee: Hast thou been worthy to judge thy fellow-man? Hast thou been so wise as to judge righteous judgment? Hast thou been so wise as to give unto him of thine own substance? Hast thou been so wise as to put aside thy foolishness? Hast thou been as one blameless - without blemish?

I ask of thee: Hast thou turned from thy childish ways? Art thou as one without "Sin"?

Ponder well these Mine Words! And answer not, ere thou hast thot well upon them!

Blameless ye shall stand before the Throne of The Most · High Living God, ere thou canst answer "Yea, Lord, I am blameless"!

So be it, there are none which deceiveth HIM; HE is as The ALL - One with ALL, and in HIM ALL are ONE. HE is not a "Thing" - yet HE is ALL that is REAL, ALL that is Eternal.

Deceive not thyself, O man. There is a Plan, a time, a place; and the time is come when ye shall bestir thyself and come forth as one prepared. Now I say, ye shall come forth - what is thine preparation? What thine qualifications? Wherein hast thou prepared thyself for to receive thine Sonship - art thou so qualified? Wherein hast thou been faithful in all things? Wherein hast thou served the Lord thy God with thine whole heart, all thine strength, all thy might? Wherein hast thou given thyself in Holy Sacrifice?

With all thine heart, all thineself thou shall serve Him. And know ye this: He hast called unto thee from out the Inner Temple - yet hast thou said: "Here I am Lord, Send Me." Send ME? I say, yea thou! I am saying: "COME!" Come all ye that have a mind - the will to serve Me, for Mine is the Greater Part.

I say: "Mine is the Greater Part." And unto thee I say: "Come! and I shall touch thee" - and no man shall call Me a liar, for I say unto thee, PROVE ME!

Let it be understood that I am not amongst the spirits of the "dead" - I am the Risen Lord. I am The One Sent of Mine Father that HIS WILL be made manifest among and in man upon the Earth this day.

Behold ME, for I stand a Living Testimony of Mine Father's Will, for I AM HIS WILL - none other do I have.

I come that ye might be found and unbound. By all the Love which is Mine I come; by the consent of the Great and Mighty Council I come; for thou art in dire need, and thou hast not known how dire thine need.

I say, thou art in dire need! So be it I KNOW! I SEE! I COME! I act according unto the Law. I know the law, and I. am come that it be fulfilled - so let it be. Aforehand I have informed thee of a Mighty Work, and ye shall see and know - as thou art prepared so shall ye be given. Ye shall increase thy capacity for understanding and love, and with all thy knowledge get understanding.

* * * * *

12

Sori Sori: This is the time of great stress for the peoples of the Earth, and We of the Council are concerned with the welfare of the people. Wherefore we come that there be great learning and that peace might be established in the Earth. Yet We labor long and without favor, without recognition, without glory amongst them.

They present themself as a pawn before us - a pawn to be won. And We weary not of our work, for We come with the consent of Our Council that this work be done, and We ask not glory or recognition as man of Earth asks.

We will that they be lifted up - that they receive of Us that which we have for them. When this is done, then we shall make known unto them that which hast been concealed from them. Then We shall show our hand, and work with them as brothers.

Be ye informed that there is no desire on Our part to withhold anything. Yet I say, they are as yet not prepared to learn that which We know. We have long been in the Schools of Great learning outside of thy own Galaxy. Thine own Galaxy is but a small part of Our learning, for We go from galaxy unto galaxy with ease, while thou art unable to traverse thine small sector of the Earth. With great ease We go from planet unto planet, with greater ease than ye go from nation to nation, for thou art a divided people. We need no passports, no great "red tape," for We are known, and we know. There is no confusion amongst us of the realms known unto us of which we belong.

There are the ones which do not deal with such as the Earth and her people - while there are ones which do. These have volunteered. These are prepared, and they know where to find the ones which are to be brot out. I say: "These are aware of them which are to be brot out."

There are no secrets unto them, for long have they been watching and waiting the time when they might step forth and assist in this work.

The hour hast now struck when great changes shall take place. There shall be Great Changes! And man shall be the ones which shall change, for he shall first change - then other changes for good shall follow.

Many have heard the Word; many have seen the Vision; many have given of themself that this be done. Now it is come when the ones which are of a mind to follow the counsel of The Council shall learn that which hast been prepared for them, for there are provisions made for each and every one so prepared. I say: "As ye are prepared so shall ye receive."

Now the ones which are sent sit in Council daily - yea, hourly - for the sole purpose of counseling thee. They are not asleep or in lethargy - they watch and wait.

Be ye as one prepared to receive them. It is given unto them to work in many ways, many ways unknown unto thee. Yet they trespass not upon thy free will. They coerce not; they boast not; they are an humble assembly. They fear not, neither do they ask alms of any man.

* * * * *

13

Let it be understood that there are ones which abide in the Earth as man which are not of the Earth - neither are they of the nether worlds.

I say, there are ones which have come into thine world as ones of another order of beings. They take up flesh as the <u>Sacrificial Robe</u>. They come that man might be lifted up; they come as one of flesh, yet they are not born of woman.

Wherein is it said that there are ones which are of another order which walk as man? When it is understood that which is said unto thee, thou shall comprehend many things which now confound and confuse thee.

There are ones from the nether world; there are ones which come from the dark regions - yet these come thru the womb of woman.

Another order comes by other means which ye know not - these are intruders! INTRUDERS!! I speak of them that ye might know that all which come are not of the Light. Fain would I speak of these - yet it is well that ye know the true from the false. Close not thine ear unto Me, for I would have ye know <u>ALL</u> things which should prepare thee for the days ahead.

I say unto thee: It is thine own salvation that ye be prepared - so let it be. Be ye not unmindful of THE MIGHTY SOURCE. Be ye not forgetful of thy part, and be ye as ones mindful of all thine blessings.

Wherein hast thy judgment been of greater importance than now? Ye shall at all times be as one informed, and ye shall be as one prepared to judge before making hasty judgment. Yet I shall give unto thee discernment and comprehension in all these matters.

Too, I say, deceive not thineself, for it is given unto men to be dreamers. They imagine great and vain imaginings, and they are not learned - they are prone to speak hastily in their vain imagings. Their vanity prompts them to speak of things they know not of. For this hast he been as a foolish child prattling his sayings. Therein is the vanity of man. He is wont to be heard and seen.

Be ye as one which KNOWS whereof ye speak. Be ye <u>in</u>-lightened, and ye shall profit therefrom/therein.

Blest is he which knows that which he says to be of the Light.

Blest is he which hast controlled his tongue.

Blest is he which knows the power of speech.

Blest is he which uses that power to glorify The Father which hast given unto him speech.

Blest is he which KNOWS the Wisdom of Silence.

* * * * *

14

By the hand of the Mighty Council hast the children of Earth been cared for. And by the Mercy of Our Father has it been so - for the children of Earth hast been a wayward lot. They have gone into darkness of their own account, and they have turned away from the Light. They have denied the Source of their being.

There are ones which have followed after them which are lost in darkness that they be reminded of their Source - that they be brot out of their darkness, their bondage. I Am Come as One of Them - Sent of Mine Father am I.

Now I bring with Me a Host which are of the mind to assist them, even unto the end. Yet many of these are not of flesh; ne'er have they been; ne'er shall they be, for it is given unto them to be of another order.

Another Order, I say. These are of another time, another place, and they are the Guardians of Greater Realms, greater peoples. They are well aware of the plight of this people of Earth. They are well aware of the conditions in which they move and have their being the people of Earth). They, too, know by what Authority they are sent forth. They ask no man aught, for they are self-sufficient, they are reliable, for they have long been prepared for this day.

Yet man knows not the Ones which are fortuned such knowledge - they are wont to think themself self-sufficient, while it is not so. They are prone to flattery and bigotry, while they are bound in darkness and bondage.

Now it is come when they shall cry out for the assistance of These which are Sent. By their assistance shall the people of the Earth be delivered out, for it is now come when the Earth hast entered into a new place upon her long journey into the unknown place of space and time. There is great danger; for I say, the Earth is the proving ground, the laboratory, and the insane asylum of the Universe. It is the place set aside as the testing ground, the School of the probationers - and for this is it called the lowest in the system.

I say, it is the School for Gods, for none less could do that which is to be done. There is a great Service to be rendered here now, and for this do We of The Great and Mighty come forth as Ones to assist. For the Earth is a much beloved and great Entity, which we shall bring thru her time of travail - and it behooves each and every child of Earth to know their part. It is a crucial time, a time of birth, a time of testing, weighing and sorting.

This is the time long foretold, when it would appear great and mysterious "things" in the skies, and the heavens shall give up their secrets. So be it, unto them which are worthy to receive, they shall be revealed.

I am speaking now for the good of All men everywhere - yet I know wherein they are which are prepared for this day for a greater work; for another place; another great revelation. I am not so foolish as to reveal the unknown mysteries unto the unprepared, the ones which would betray their trust and themself.

I place before them a plan, and they shall see but part, for no man seeth in toto the completeness of such plans of which I speak, for they comprehend not the whole. For the whole concerns many a world; many a people; many systems of worlds; people of greater orders than the Earthians.

Lo, it is come when the sabers shall rattle in thy closets and the hearth stones shall be cold and the wheat shall be no more. The land shall be desolate, and the mother shall weep for her unborn - so be it she shall wail loud and sorely for her unborn! She shall ask deliverance for her children's children, and she shall perish with them.

* * * * *

15

Sori Sori: Say unto them: They shall fear the law. They shall account for themself, for their deeds. They shall bring up their children to be accountable for <u>themself</u>. They shall bring them up in the way of righteousness and forget not that I am come that they be made responsible!

I say unto them: For this did I come; for this I AM COME; for this do I give unto thee the Law. It is exact, and each and every mortal comes under the law which I give unto them.

When one comes into the Earth - takes upon self garments of flesh - he hast made a covenant with Me, and he comes for a purpose. For the purpose is he allowed to enter into the world of form, yet he forgets the purpose - therein is the pity!

He goes in and out of flesh as the unknowing one. He forgets from whence he came – neither whither he goeth. Yet he hast been told aforehand - he hast read his records aforehand. He hast two ways to go - and wherein hast he found his way back? For that matter, he is lost. He hast become confused and bewildered. He hast followed many strange gods.

Now I come, even as of old, declaring this is the New Day, the time of the end. Ye shall hear Me this day! For I am not to be put aside; I am not to be mocked - neither am I to be put aside or cast out!

I say, it is the time and the place to be about Mine Father's business - for this hast HE sent Me - for this am I speaking unto thee.

Ye shall remember well that which I say, for it is most personal. I speak unto thee, O Reader; I speak unto each and every one which hast a mind, an ear, and I bid thee come forth this day and prepare thineself. For it cometh soon when ye shall go forth into a strange land, and ye shall find therein that which shall be strange unto thee. It shall be new, and it behooves Me to tell thee that there is no death. Ye shall find that ye shall step from thine worn garment into another more fitting. And is it not said many times: "As ye are prepared so shall ye receive"? It is the law.

Weary not of Mine sayings - yet ye have not comprehended them. Listen unto Me; give ear and I shall give unto thee comprehension, for there is a part for thee, and for this ye shall be prepared.

I Am He which knows wherein thou art bound, and I am come that ye be unbound. Yet thou hast first to do that which is required of thee. And it is clearly stated, that ye shall walk in the way of the Lord. Ye shall comply with the law which I give unto thee, and <u>then</u> I shall do My part.

* * * * *

16

Be ye as one prepared, for at no time shall ye enter into the Holy of Holies unprepared. Thy past glories shall be of no account. Thine vainglory shall be of no account, for all thy vanity shall be as the legirons which shall bind thee.

I say, put aside all thine pride; all thine pettiness; all thine hatred, intolerance; all thine foolishness, and be ye alert and watchful. Hear ye Me, and I shall speak unto thee of things profitable unto thee.

Forget not that I Am He which is Sent. I come as The Father's Will made manifest in Me. I come as thy Benefactor, as thy Counselor, as the forerunner of that which ye shall become. I say: Follow ye Me and I shall lead thee out of bondage. Fear not! Follow ye Me. I shall deal justly with thee, and no man shall call Me a fraud and imposter, for I shall prove Mineself.

Be ye aware of them which hold out their hand asking alms of thee, that they receive their reward for "the Word," for no price is put on Mine Word. I say I give freely. I ask naught of thee save obedience unto the law. Therefore, I say unto thee: Ye shall first receive Mine Servants even as ye would receive Me. Then I shall honor thee, for thou hast in like manner received Me and Mine servant. Honor first Mine servant - then I shall remember thee.

* * * * *

17

Sori Sori: By the hand of the Great and Divine Council shall ye be given this part of Counsel. It shall be for the good of all - yet there are ones which shall refuse it - unto them is given the lesser part; unto them which receive it is given the Greater Part. When they have rejected it, they shall be as the ones left unto the lesser parts - they shall wait for the greater.

Now ye shall send forth this part as that which hast been given unto thee. Ask of them no penny, and be ye as one prepared for the next part. There shall be a next part and it, too, shall go unto them in the same manner. For this is it given unto thee in parts. They shall ponder well each part, and remember well that which is said herein in these parts.

It is given unto Me to observe them and to know that which they do with it. Therefore, I say unto them: Be ye thotful of Me and of Mine counsel. I am apt at this, and I, for that matter, have been at this for a long while. Therefore, I know what I am about.

For this time I give unto thee these letters, and they shall be as personal letters unto YE, the Reader. Each shall receive it in his own way and interpret it in his own tongue. None shall place his own interpretation upon it for another. Each shall find herein hidden that which another may not find, for I shall do a strange thing - I shall hide up Mine Word from the unjust and the imprudent, while I shall show the just and humble that which is hidden from the unjust. Therefore I say: Watch ye with diligence; read ye with eyes that see; and be ye alert unto that which ye see.

It is now come when I shall seek out the ones which are prepared to go all the way with Me. I am come that they be found and gathered in - blest shall they be.

Now think ye not that I am not a person - for hast not Mine Father given unto Me personality? Think ye that I am a figment of man's mind? Hast his mind deluded him in this?

I am as the Eternal Son of God. Bear ye in mind, I AM Sent of HIM, The SOURCE of thy BEing, that ye might know thine Eternal Source and Self, for that is the Real, the Eternal, while flesh is but the mortal garment, temporary at best, fleeting. And it perishes even as all mortal material, for it goes back into the substance from whence it came.

I speak unto thee of the duality, the two-fold personality. There is the two-fold - ye know the one of flesh, yet ye but dream of the other which is as a "hope," as a dream. Yet I say unto thee: Ye are not flesh - flesh but hides thine innermost Self, thine true identity.

Think ye not that I know ye by flesh. I know thine true identity, for I see that which ye know not - that which is forever thine mark, thine very Self, which is the same yesterday and forever. This is the Light which never fails. I come that it might not be hidden within the flesh.

It is said: "Let thine Light shine forth that all might see it" - it is for this that I come, that ye the sleeper might come forth and KNOW thineself to be alive. Fashion for thyself no legiron. Bring thineself unto me as a little child - as a living sacrifice - in humility and readiness to receive Me as I AM. Ask of no man his blessings, his opinions, his favors. Give unto Me credit for being that which I AM - then I shall give unto thee in Greater capacity.

* * * *

18

Before we continue, let it be understood that there are ones within flesh which hast the power and the authority to speak for Me - in Mine Name. For this have I ordained them as Mine Voice, Mine hands made manifest. Therefore, I put Mine Words into their mouth and they speak them. As the Will of Mine Father, they are put into the mouth of Mine priests and priestesses.

For that matter, I AM the Will of Mine Father, and I give unto Mine servants the power and the authority to speak in Mine name.

By the power and the authority invested in Me, I have ordained this, Mine Priestess, that she might do this Mine Work which I have allotted unto her. For this have I prepared her, for she hast been a faithful and willing servant.

I speak the WORD, she hears and obediently she performs the work I give unto her. She fears no man; she gives no quarter, neither does she take any. Blame not Mine servant that this paper compares not to the learned letters of the intellectuals, for it is not Mine intention to give unto thee a great and lengthy treatise of philosophy or science. And I have no intention to dwell on personalities. I am come that ye be lifted up - that ye might be as one prepared to receive of the greater mysteries. So be it that I am prepared to give unto thee as ye are prepared to receive. Yet it is not yet time to reveal unto thee the "Greater Mysteries" which are neither written or spoken.

I say: The "Greater Mysteries" are neither spoken or written.

* * * * *

19

Sori Sori: Be ye blest this day, and be ye as the hand of Me made manifest unto them and say unto them in Mine name that the way is prepared before them, and at no time have they been given the bitter cup. For that matter, they have prepared the bitter cup for themself - it is not of Me.

I am not prepared to give unto them the cup of Living Water. It is said: The time is now come when they shall choose which way they go - it is so.

I say, "Come follow ME" - yet there are ones which sit as the poor in Spirit, moving not. They are as the dead - they hear not, neither do they stir.

For this do I say, Awaken! Awaken!! Bestir thyself! Come forth and follow Me. Wherein have they stirred?

I am the One which sees them in their lethargy and in their sleep. It is a pitiful sight I see, for they know not that they stand on the brink of danger! I say "Danger!" I repeat: "They are in danger!"

They shall be faced with great peril, for all is not well with them. This is the time to awaken. This is the time to be up and about their preparation, for they shall enter into a place wherein they have not been, wherein there shall be great turmoil for the ones unprepared. There shall be much confusion for the unprepared, the unstable, the poor in Spirit, the ones which hast not been as the fortunate ones - the ones which have had the fortune to know that which is prepared before them.

The Parable

I say: A table is prepared before thee. On that table is many things (and that is not a mistake on My part). I say: ON that table "IS" many things, and each shall be his own porter. He shall find on that table a portion which he is prepared to receive, for he hast created his own appetite. His own mind is prepared to find that which he hast fortuned unto himself. Therefore, he shall find his own place, his own environment - and he shall in no wise be the better for his opinions, his lusts, his cravings. He shall find they have profited him naught.

Yet he which puts away the passions, hate, lust and opinions, his pettiness, hypocrisy and malice, and follows where I lead, shall find thereon the fruit of Eternal Life.

* * * * *

El Pater

20

Sori Sori: Hast it not been said that great Light shall be shed upon the Earth? It is so - So shall it be. Now it is come when one shall go forth as one prepared, and he shall go as one in full armor. He shall walk with men; he shall counsel men; and he shall bless them with his presence. He shall carry with him the rod of power and authority, for I shall give unto him the authority and the power to speak in Mine Name. And he shall be as one submissive unto Mine will, remembering always that I am the Will of Mine Father made manifest.

For this have prepared him - for this have I called him forth and given unto him the name, which is El Pater. This shall be his new name, and no man shall be unto him a barrier, neither shall they put him to shame, for he shall Honor The Father, and he shall be just in all his dealings. He shall fare well, for I shall deal justly with him, and he shall remember from whence his calling. He shall be as one mindful of the call, and he shall at no time betray himself.

He shall begin his ministry now, and he shall waver not, for I have set Mine Seal upon him. I shall give unto him a number which shall be put within the palm of his hand, and it shall signify the number of days which are within the time left for the work at hand. Yet no man shall decipher the meaning thereof, for I speak unto thee of the mysteries which no man can understand at this time - yet it shall be revealed unto him in the time to come. Wherein is it said, There is a time unto all things? I say: There is a season unto all things, a time of learning, a time of teaching, a time of going out, a time of coming in. So be it there is a time of light, a time of darkness, plowing and sowing. So be it that there is more to be said on that, yet it behooves thee to note that which I have said - ponder well Mine Words.

Ye shall make known that which I have said to El Pater, and he shall be alert and prepare himself, for the time draws nigh when I shall call him forth as one prepared to do a mighty work, and he shall do it with joy and gladness - so be it and Selah.

21

Sori Sori: This day I would give unto thee this Word, and it shall be for the good of all - so be it and Selah.

Fortune thyself to hear me, and I shall give unto thee that which I have kept for thee, for thine own reward is kept for thee. Thou knowest not that which I have kept for this day. When ye shall be as one prepared to receive it, it is that which thou hast not as yet dreamed nor asked.

So be it I am prepared to give it, yet there is work to be done ere ye become one of the porters within the place of Mine abode. How-be-it thou hast gone out from Mine place, and it is said, Ye shall return - so be it and Selah.

Hold out thine hand and I shall touch it, and ye shall receive of Me that which I have for them, and it shall profit them to receive it in Mine Name - for this is Mine time. Mine Word shall go out, and unto them which receiveth the WORD, unto them shall I show Mine hand. I shall touch them and they shall know Mine touch.

So be it I am not lacking in judgment, I am not lacking in wisdom, neither mercy or Love, for Mine Love compares only to Mine Father's which hast Sent Me. They know not the wisdom of Mine actions in this - they comprehend not the judgment of Mine acts, the mercy which I have upon them. I say: Mine acts are three-fold; Mine Words are three-fold; and the Mighty Council hast prepared a part for each and every one which partakes of Mine Word. They but have to accept it in Mine Name and abide by it. Then they shall bear testimony of Me, and they shall likewise be obedient unto the law. They shall be as one with each other. They shall not deny Mine "Servant" which hast been My diligent handmaiden.

These are the things which I would place before thee this day, and I say unto thee, Mine Reader: Thou art not exempt from the law, no matter under which banner thou hast labored, for thou art not as yet come into the fullness of thine estate. Thou hast not as yet finished thine sojourn. So be ye not puffed up. Wear thine laurels not in peace - with satisfaction – for they deceive Me not.

I know that which thou hast done; I know that which is to do, and I come that it be done. Rebel not against Me, neither Mine manner - resist not that which I bring forth in Wisdom. Judge not Mine Servants by that which I give unto them to do, for I am responsible for Mine own acts - require from them obedience, not perfection in all things!

I take the obedience and use them as the Chalice that I might fill it to the full that ye, Mine Reader, might be blest. Think ye well upon this, for wherein hast thou heard Mine Voice and followed Me? Wherein hast thou prepared thineself to do Mine work? Thinkest thou I do not know thee?

It is said: "The harvest is great and the reapers few." I say unto thee THIS DAY: The time is come when ye shall bow down thineself in holy supplication and obedience, and willingness to do the Will of the Father - ye shall surrender up thyself and falter not. So be it I shall be thine witness, and no man shall deny thee thine inheritance, for I am the Keeper and the Guardian thereof.

* * * * *

22

Sori Sori: By the Grace of Mine Father and by the efforts and Divine Director hast this Great and Mighty Council been set up. It is for the purpose of serving the Light - for the purpose of giving forth the law, which is the Eternal Verities.

I am One of The Council. For that matter, I am Head of The Council, and it is said that there are numerous lodges and sub-councils within or under the Supreme Council.

While men of Earth know little of the working of the Great and Mighty Council, they have set up their councils as poor imitations - as the lesser - for they know not the power, the ethic, the responsibility, which goes with such as I speak of. When I speak of the "Great and Mighty Council," It is the Organ thru which All the Work for the system of planets is accomplished, thru and by the combined efforts of a dedicated Company of <u>Personalities</u> - yea, I say Personalities.

While there are ones which would deny Us personality, I say We do have personality and individuality, with the Will (Combined Will) to serve the Light which never fails. So be it I come as a member of this Council, in humility and with great Love and Wisdom.

I come with great compassion for suffering humanity; the ones which are groping in darkness; the ones which have become lost in the maze of thinking; and the forest which hold them bound. They see not, for the shadows of the past hang deeply about them. They lose their way; in the depth of despair they cry out, and I hear their cries - yet I reach out Mine hand, and they are so feeble of Spirit they reach not out to touch it.

They sit in judgment on their fellow men, while they do nothing to lift them up - they forget from whence comes their help. They take, giving no thot unto the ones which stand guard over them.

This is the school of preparation, yet they refuse that which is placed before them. They ask of men their opinions, their blessings, and their alms, while all that is within Our Power We do that they might become self-sufficient - I say: "THAT THEY BECOME SELF-SUFFICIENT" - that they might come into maturity, awaken unto their own potentials and become Sons of God. This is offered unto each and every one which is capable of Eternal Life.

Now it is come when the very gates of Heaven shall open up unto the ones prepared to enter therein. There shall be a great awakening! For this am I come; for this am I speaking; for this shall I speak - I shall be heard!!

Now ye which hear Me and give unto Me credit for being that which I am, shall come to know Me and to bear witness of Me, for I shall keep Mine Word - I shall not betray Mineself nor Mine trust. Ye shall listen and I shall speak - yet I say, deceive not thineself, for I am not a petty priest; I am not a foolish nun - I am a serious man; I am not a false god. So I say unto thee: Be aware of Me, and I shall give unto thee that which shall profit thee. I shall stand guard at thy gate, when thou hast cast aside thine puny ways and thine conceit, thine opinions and offensive ways that ye be prepared for Mine Part.

I bow unto no man; I ask of none favors. Yet I bow unto the Light in every man - that which is Eternal within him. I grovel not in the pit; I pray not unto any man that I receive sustenance from him - I KNOW wherein I am staid. Therefore, I say unto thee: Look, and behold The

Son of God. Be ye even as He - and cast not lots for His garments, for they are even as naught unto thee. I say: Look ye well unto thine own. Purify thineself that ye might walk the way in which I go, and this shall profit thee, for I shall bring thee into the place wherein I abide - therein is no darkness, no bondage. Yet I say unto thee, I am not favored. I am not favored - I am The One which hast become that which I wast created for to BE. So be it, and it is SO - so shall it ever BE.

* * * * *

23

Sori Sori: Such is Mine Word unto thee this day – for this Mine Word shall go forth that all might know that which I say. Mine Word precedes Me - where it is accepted in Mine Name there I am. The Word goes out before Me that they might be prepared for to receive Me.

This is Mine Plan which no man can pilfer; neither shall he abort it, for he knows not that which I shall do. I shall do a new and strange thing which shall confound the ones which are not prepared to receive Me.

The way is prepared, and I come as a "thief in the night" while they sleep - and yet they sleep, knowing not the plan, neither of Mine coming. They go about asking of men their opinions, seeking of men their counsel while I say: Come! Listen! Hear that which I say! Yet they hear Me not - they listen not!

Bear in mind, I give not of Mineself unto the unjust, the imprudent - I give unto them which seek that which I have for them. I bless them which seek Me out, which seek the Light which I AM.

There are ones which are now within the Earth (at this time) which are prepared to give unto thee the Cup of Living Water, and I am One of Them. Be ye as one prepared to receive - let it be, so shall it be.

Forget not that the way hast been made strait before thee, and it is now come when ye shall follow in Mine footsteps - and ye shall taste of the fruit of Eternal Life. That is Mine Word for this day - So be it I shall speak again and again.

* * * * *

The Test

24

Sori Sori: Fortune thineself this part and it shall be placed within the foregoing letters, for they shall see and know that which I say unto thee.

There are many which say this and that, each adding his own opinion and embellishment. Yet I have said unto thee, ye shall not add one word or take away one word - ye shall give it unto them as ye receive it, and nothing shall be given unto them without the consent of the Mighty Council.

For it is now come when many shall come forth declaring they are sent - yet I say, they shall prove themself. Yet no man shall demand of them proof, for they shall not satisfy man's demands for proof.

Man shall find his proof in the word and deed. Yet he shall find that his deeds shall live after him and his works shall be a living monument unto him, for he shall be as the one which hast been unto himself true.

Man shall demand proof; they shall look unto thee for proof - yet I say: He shall find none, for he shall not be satisfied. Man shall test the Word by application of the law. He shall test that which I say by application of the law. For this is the test I ask of him; this is his test; and ye shall exact none, for he shall test himself and grade himself according unto his preparation.

None shall sit in judgment of him - neither shall any man sit in judgment of Me or Mine Work, for I Am He which hast come that he might know wherein he is staid. So be it I bring with Me a Mighty Host, and they shall be as ones prepared for any and all occasions - so be it and Selah.

* * * * *

25

Sori Sori: Say unto them which ask that there are ones which would distress them for the sake of bringing about the notice which they are apt to desire. I say: There is great danger and stress. Yet I ask that it be given unto them that they be prepared, for this is the whole desire of the Company of which I am part.

The ones which <u>would be</u> the prophet is but the ono which knows not - the one which hast caused much fear and anxiety.

I say unto thee: I KNOW, and I see that which the <u>would-be</u> prophet sees not, for Mine vantage point is the Greater One. Prepare thyself for changes, for changes are the order of the day. Change is progress, and progress is change. So be it that there is no progress without change.

For this do I say: "Prepare thyself for the Greater Part - prepare thyself for change." Be ye as one which can welcome change, and fortune thyself the new part, ever changing. And waste not thine time looking backward, for say unto thee, there are greater things in store than thou hast known; there are greater things prepared for thee than thou hast ever had; there are heights undreamed of - yet attainable.

Yet I say: Ye shall not look back, for to look back is to stumble. There is a parable which says: "Turn not back lest thou turn to a pillar of salt." Know ye the meaning of that? While it is a simple saying, it behooves thee to ponder well its meaning.

Blest Is He.

Be ye as one pliable, acceptable unto Me, and I shall lead thee into greater heights, greener pastures - greater glories shall be thine. Ask not for small favors - bless thyself, for I say: Blest is he which follows after Me; blest is he which goes where I go; blest is he which goes all the way with Me; blest is he which falters not; blest is he which hast received his inheritance. Blest is he which hast upon his head the Crown and within his hand the Orb and the Scepter, for he hast overcome.

* * * * *

26

By the counsel of the Great and Mighty Council shall they be prepared for the Greater Counsel. They ask of men; yet I say, they receive not the greater from men, for men have not the power to open up the floodgates of knowledge unto them. For the greater comes not by word - neither the written pages.

Not all their books contain the knowledge, wisdom, the learning which can be conveyed in one instant in and by the manner in which We reveal the secrets which are so mysterious unto them which seek.

The Failure or Success of Prayer

Yet they seek - they ask of whom? They look, but where? They say this and that, but what does it avail them? Not all their mantrams hast made them wise - neither hast their decrees cleansed them. For the most part they pray unto a false god, an unknown god. Wherein hast it been said: "They know not their Source"?

When they call out in the name of The All-Wise, All-Powerful Father selflessly, they shall be answered.

I say: Pray ye not to be heard of men or to receive their favor; pray ye that all men be lifted up -so be it ye shall be heard.

Now ye shall be as ones prepared to receive of the Greater Mysteries, for it is now come when they shall be revealed unto the just and the prudent.

I say: Behold ye the Hand of God move. See it move, and know ye that it moves, for by the Hand of God shall these things be revealed unto thee. This is the day of Revelation - the Revelation of Revelations, wherein ye shall have understanding of all former Revelations. For this have I put within thine hand these things of former ages. Age after age there hast been given revelation after revelation - yet not understood.

While I say unto thee this day, there shall now be understanding of the "<u>former</u>" Revelations. So let there be understanding and wisdom.

* * * * *

27

How-be-it that there are ones amongst thee which know not that I am come? They have looked for One which would come in a cloud. How-be-it that they do not perceive the cloud? How-be-it they think there is no cloud??

I say: I AM COME! even in the "Cloud"! While I say, I AM HERE, the cloud is heavy and they know neither! They see not, for the cloud is dense and their eyes blinded! Yea, blind and deaf art they, for they see not -- neither do they hear. While the Word is placed before them, it is not comprehended.

I am speaking that they might have comprehension. I shall speak unto them in ways which are new and strange. I shall write upon their heart that which they shall not forget. I shall do a wondrous thing, and I shall be as the Author and Finisher of Mine Work, for no man shall abort the Plan of which I speak.

I am the Host of Hosts, and I bring with Me mighty warriors, long trained in the way of the just and prudent. I know them to be trustworthy, and they are Mighty, endowed with power and Wisdom!

They have not taken up residence upon the Earth; they are free from all bonds, all bounds. They are bound by no law save that of "Love," which motivates their every act. They know the Earth - all the systems of Earth, man, animal, plants, yea - the thots of every one. Every living thing they know well. They know the composition of all things - I say, there are no secrets, for they are learned in their part; they are learned in the schools far beyond man's comprehension, and at no time shall man put them to shame.

I tell thee of a truth - they art thy Superiors. Think ye not that thou art wise, O man! For thou art lower than the "Angels." Thou hast as yet not seen that which ye shall become, for thou art within a "low grade," and I say unto thee: "Come forth" - and ye move not, for thou art in lethargy.

I stand ready to assist thee when ye pick up thine feet and reach out thy hand that I might touch it - be ye not deceived in this - I say, "Try Me." I say: Pick up thy feet; seek Me out; look unto Me; ask of Me. Be ye as one Selfless, and I shall walk with thee all the way.

I give not Mineself unto the unjust and imprudent. I bow down unto the just and prudent. I go not into the den of the dragon; yet I go down into the bottomless pit to find the just and the humble. I bow down unto the ones which give of themself that others be lifted up.

I give not unto the bigot and braggart, for they find their reward in the plaudits of men. They find their reward in man's flattery - and wherein hast it profited them? I say unto them: "Thou fool, what hast it profited thee?" I am come that ye be not deceived of men, for their flattery is liken unto the tack in thine shoe.

Blest art they which shun man's flattery and finds his reward in selfless service, asking naught of man - yea, such is the reward of the Servant, the reward which is everlasting and outshining a King's diadem, is that which I offer thee. I say: Come follow ye Me and I shall show thee many things which thou hast not seen.

I promise thee not fame nor fortune; I promise thee freedom, even as I am free. Think ye that I am an impostor, asking of thee favor? I say unto thee: I bow down Mineself that ye be lifted up! So be it that ye shall give unto Me credit for being that which I AM, and I shall show unto thee that which thou hast not seen. I promise thee not miracles; I promise thee Eternal Freedom - this shall profit thee. Wherein hast there been a man amongst thee which hast given unto thee that which delivered thee? I say there hast not been one. Even though he hast been as one mild and gentle, he hast not been unto thee the deliverer; he hast not been unto thee Savior. I say: To save thyself is the greater wisdom.

A man goeth unto the rescue of a drowning man and knoweth not how to swim, perisheth also. So be it I say: First pick up thine own feet, and they shall be shown the way, for I have opened up the way - and for this am I the Way-Shower.

Place thine hand in Mine and I shall lead thee gently and I shall deal justly with thee, for I know thine needs, thine frailties. Yet I say; Ye shall overcome thine weakness, for shall give unto thee as thou art prepared to receive.

* * * * *

28

Let this go down in history as I have spoken it, for it is spoken for a reason and a time. This shall conclude "The Part of Counsel," and We shall enter it into the records. Therefore, they shall have it available as they are prepared to receive it. Then another shall follow this part, "The Part of Counsel." This next part shall be "The Part of Wisdom," and it shall profit them to accept it in Mine Name, for I say: As they accept Mine Word and Mine Servant, so do they receive Me.

I say: Bear ye in mind, I AM HE which is sent to bear witness of Mine Father. Likewise do I send Mine Word out by Mine Servants, that they bear witness of Me. Unto them which receive them in Mine Name I say: Behold ye Me, and I shall touch thee and ye shall be quickened, and ye shall know as I know.

Bear ye in mind that I am bound by Mine Word, and Mine Word is valid - no man shall invalidate it. So be it I am come that it be brot forth this day the plan which is given unto Me - and I shall do Mine part. Let it be said thou hast done thine.

Let it be said: Thou hast been true unto thine trust. Blest art they which are trustworthy.

Blest art they which are prepared to receive Me. Blest art they which are with Me. Blest art they which go all the way with Me. So be it I shall give unto them as I have received of Mine Father, for He hast empowered Me with the Authority to give unto thee just as I have received - and I have received Mine Inheritance in full. So be it and Selah.

This concludes "The Part of Counsel."

* * * *

Recorded by Sister Thedra

www.ingramcontent.com/pod-product-compliance
Lightning Source LLC
LaVergne TN
LVHW051516070426
835507LV00023B/3140